Soap Opera
Quiz Book

Chris Bradshaw

First published in 2008 by Collins
An imprint of **HarperCollins*Publishers***
77-85 Fulham Palace Road
Hammersmith, London
W6 8JB

www.collins.co.uk

Copyright © HarperCollinsPublishers Ltd 2008

The Sun and *Sun* are registered trademarks of
News Group Newspapers Ltd

ISBN 978-0-00-727080-4

A catalogue record for this book is available from the
British Library

Introduction

Who did Tracy Barlow get to lie under oath at her court case? What was *Brookside's* Thomas Sweeney better known as? Who killed Dirty Den? Which Neighbour had a hit with *It Make You Feel Good*? Find the answers to these and many more soap opera teasers in *The Sun Soap Opera Quiz Book*.

You'll find questions on *Coronation Street*, *EastEnders*, *Emmerdale*, *Hollyoaks*, *Home and Away* and *Neighbours* as well as old favourites like *Brookside*, *Crossroads*, *Dallas* and *Dynasty*. We've even thrown in *Prisoner Cell Block H*.

With 100 unique categories featuring anything and everything from the babes and bad boys, hunks and grumps to births, marriages and deaths we've got the whole of the soap world covered. There's something for everyone from the new viewer to the dedicated soap fanatic.

So, if you think you know your Annie Walkers from your Dot Cottons, your Andy Sugdens from your Paul Robinsons, you've come to the right place.

As Jim McDonald would say 'It's time to get cracking, so it is'.

Enjoy.

Contents

Coronation Street The Early Years

1 Ena Sharples was a caretaker at which mission?

2 What was Valerie Barlow's maiden name?

3 Jed Stone was a lodger with Minnie Caldwell but what did she always call him: M'laddo, Sunny Jim or Cheeky?

4 How did Ken Barlow's mother Ida meet her death?

5 Who in 1964 died in the snug of the Rovers Return?

6 Which pop singer played Len Fairclough's son Stanley?

7 Who said 'I've had trouble with fellas since I was four years old'?

8 True or false: Betty first started serving at the Rovers in 1969?

9 Which three characters were likened to Macbeth's three witches?

10 Who was Alf Roberts's consort when he became Mayor of Weatherfield in 1973?

11 How did Harry Hewitt die?

Answers on page 204

12 What was the occupation of Betty's husband Cyril?

13 Ena Sharples was famous for always drinking what in the Rovers?

14 Ken Barlow turned down the offer of a teaching job in which country after the death of Valerie: Australia, Jamaica or New Zealand?

15 Which character made her Street debut as a bridesmaid at Emily and Ernest Bishop's wedding: Rita, Mavis or Phyllis Pearce?

16 Elsie Tanner worked in which shop alongside Dot Greenhalgh?

17 Who was jilted by Gordon Clegg just a week before they were due to be married?

18 Who did Alf Roberts marry in 1978: Renee Bradshaw, Veronica Bradshaw or Stephanie Bradshaw?

19 What was hanging on Hilda Ogden's wall before the flying ducks?

20 Ray Langton fled to which country after the birth of Tracy: Germany, Holland or Belgium?

Answers on page 204

Coronation Street
The 1980s

1 Who became a CB Radio enthusiast with the unlikely handle of Slim Jim?

2 What was the name of Fred Gee's wife: Eunice, Elizabeth or Edie?

3 Len and Rita Fairclough fostered which young tomboy?

4 Mavis Riley fell for which fellow night school student?

5 Which Street resident unwittingly married a bigamist?

6 Elsie Tanner left Weatherfield to start a new life in which country?

7 Darren Whatley stabbed and killed which street heart-throb?

8 Whose alter ego was Vince St Clair?

9 Who briefly left her husband to live in a theatrical boarding house and work as a cabaret singer?

10 Ivy Tilsley was a devout follower of which religion?

11 Which *Coronation Street* resident owned a budgie called Randy?

12 Who beat Alf Roberts by seven votes to become a Weatherfield councillor in 1987?

13 Hilda Ogden won a raffle where the prize was a date with which Weatherfield romeo?

14 Where did Derek Wilton propose to Mavis: on a trip to Paris, on one knee in the Rovers or through The Kabin letterbox?

15 Who left Weatherfield for Australia after winning a fortune on a five horse accumulator?

16 What was the name of Alan Bradley's daughter?

17 Who left Curly Watts shortly after throwing an unwanted surprise party for him?

18 Pensioner Harry Ashton had what unlikely job: nanny, paperboy or hairdresser?

19 What did Curly Watts, Eddie Yeats and Chalkie Whiteley have in common?

20 Harry Clayton had what occupation: milkman, window cleaner or road sweeper?

Answers on page 204

Coronation Street
The 1990s

1 What was Fiona Middleton's occupation?

2 Which youngster set fire to her kitchen after being left home alone: Sarah Platt, Tracy Barlow or Rosie Webster?

3 What was Fred Elliott's middle name: Handel, Mozart or Elgar?

4 Who famously used to refer to Derek Wilton as Dirk?

5 Reg Holdsworth arranged for which Street resident to win the Bettabuys trolley dash?

6 Which eco-warrior led the protest against the development of the Red Rec?

7 Deirdre's husband Samir came from which country?

8 What was the name of the dating agency run by Alec Gilroy?

9 Who was forced to drink in the Rovers with no trousers on after losing a bet with his wife that he could shave off Kevin Webster's moustache?

10 Which pair eloped to Scotland in 1998?

Answers on page 204

11 Emily Bishop opened which charity shop: The Friends of Weatherfield Hospital, The Friends of Weatherfield Comprehensive or The Friends of the Red Rec?

12 Who did Don Brennan try to frame when he burnt down Baldwin's factory?

13 Which member of the McDonald family became addicted to gambling?

14 Who was the area manager of Bettabuys: Brendan Scott, Terry Scott or Ronnie Scott?

15 Who had affairs with both Steve and Jim McDonald?

16 Which unlikely pair have both posed nude for art classes?

17 True or false: Brewery Newton and Ridley tried to turn the Rovers into a theme pub called Yankees?

18 Zoe Tattersall was lured into which dodgy cult?

19 Deirdre fell for fraudster Jon Lindsay. What did he pretend was his occupation?

20 Lorraine Brownlow and Linda Sykes scrapped for the attention of which man at the 1999 Valentine's disco?

Answers on page 204

Coronation Street
The Modern Era

1 Who left Weatherfield and headed to Las Vegas after inheriting a valuable antique?

2 What is the name of Tony Gordon's bitchy ex-wife?

3 The discovery of what caused the evacuation of number four Coronation Street: a skeleton, a leaking gas pipe or an unexploded bomb?

4 The pupils of Weatherfield Comprehensive performed which musical?

5 Who fell for what he thought was a foreign beauty called Shania, little knowing that Shania was really a man?

6 Who did Tracy Barlow get to lie under oath during her court case?

7 How did Paul Connor die: car crash, run over by a tram or stabbed at a nightclub?

8 What was the name of the Polish worker who died at the Underworld factory?

9 Who was responsible for the death of Michelle Connor's lover Dean?

10 What is the name of Violet Wilson's sister?

11 Becky Granger went joyriding in whose Morris Minor?

12 Norris, Ivor and George battled for the affections of which woman?

13 Who held a false wake to see what her friends really thought of her?

14 Rosie Webster had an affair with which schoolteacher?

15 Who set fire to the Peacocks' house?

16 Where did Sarah and Jason Grimshaw go for their honeymoon?

17 Who faked his own death in an attempt to ruin Sarah Lou's wedding day?

18 Whose stash of drugs did David Platt hide in Bethany's doll?

19 Which actress who plays a glamorous granny on the Street, celebrated her 50th birthday in April 2007?

20 Hayley Cropper left *Coronation Street* to do charity work in which country: Mexico, Moldova or Mozambique?

Answers on page 204

Around Weatherfield

QUIZ 5

1 What is the name of the Italian restaurant owned by Leanne Battersby?

2 True or false: *Coronation Street's* taxi firm is called Fleet Cars?

3 What is the name of *Coronation Street's* newsagent shop?

4 Who worked as a caretaker at Weatherfield Comprehensive: Derek Wilton, Curly Watts or Terry Duckworth?

5 What is the name of the cafe owned by Roy Cropper?

6 Diggory Compton owned what type of shop: butcher, baker or candlestick maker?

7 True or false: *Coronation Street* was going to be called Florizel Street?

8 What is the name of Weatherfield's local primary school: Bessie Street, Billy Street or Broad Street?

9 Weatherfield's supermarket is called: Bettabuys, Cheaperbuys or Whoateallthebuys?

10 Who was Kevin Webster's first boss at the garage?

Answers on page 204

11 What is the name of Weatherfield's local football team: City, United or County?

12 Which pair opened a hardware store called D&S Hardware?

13 What was the name of Mike Baldwin's lingerie factory?

14 Karl Foster worked at which Weatherfield institution?

15 What was the name of the newspaper edited by Ken Barlow: The Recorder, The Bugle or The Tribune?

16 Who owned the Corner Shop and also became mayor of Weatherfield?

17 Which character left the delights of Weatherfield for Lytham St Annes in 1980: Elsie Tanner, Hilda Ogden or Ena Sharples?

18 What is the name of the 'posh end' of Weatherfield: Oakhill, Elmhill or Yewhill?

19 Mike Baldwin used to the own the garage. What did he call it?

20 What is the name of the chip shop on Rosamund Street: Wong's, Wang's or Chang's?

Answers on page 204

The Women of Coronation Street

1 Who is the owner of *Coronation Street's* hair salon?

2 Who famously smoked her cigarettes in a long black holder, Lady Penelope style?

3 What were the names of Deirdre's three husbands?

4 Who was the first regular black character on *Coronation Street*?

5 Spider was the nephew of which long standing Weatherfield resident?

6 In what decade did Betty Turpin start working at the Rovers: 1960s, 1970s or 1980s?

7 The top rated episode of *Coronation Street* featured the departure of which well loved character?

8 Who said 'we don't need sewers round here when we've got Ena Sharples'?

9 Derek Wilton and Victor Pendlebury battled for the attention of which Weatherfield newsagent?

10 What was Hayley Cropper's maiden name?

11 What was Doreen Fenwick's unlikely former occupation: nun, trapeze artist or exotic dancer?

12 Who got pregnant by her gay best friend?

13 What was the name of Minnie Caldwell's cat: Bobby, Denis or George?

14 What was Sally's maiden name before she married Kevin Webster?

15 The millionaire fiancé of which Rovers barmaid had a gay affair?

16 Who first met her husband after he drove past her and soaked her with a puddle: Sally Webster, Vera Duckworth or Gail Platt?

17 Which motorcyclist became a barmaid at the Rovers?

18 In 1982, which *Coronation Street* character was voted the fourth most recognised woman in Britain: Bet Lynch, Hilda Ogden or Annie Walker?

19 Actress Nikki Sanderson played which *Coronation Street* hairdresser?

20 Which *Coronation Street* star was the first soap actress to have a Top 40 hit?

Answers on page 205

Coronation Street Deaths

QUIZ 7

1 Valerie Barlow was electrocuted after using what faulty electrical device?

2 The husband of which long term Weatherfield resident was killed in a wages snatch at Baldwin's factory?

3 How did Alan Bradley die?

4 Who died at Ken and Deirdre's second wedding reception?

5 How did Richard Hillman die?

6 Dennis Stringer died in a car crash while taking which friend to hospital?

7 Who was stabbed to death outside a nightclub?

8 Who killed Tommy Harris by smashing him over the head with a wrench?

9 Des Barnes was beaten to death by a gang of drug dealers while trying to protect his stepson. What was his name?

10 Renee Roberts died while learning to do what: fly, drive or ballroom dance?

11 Who died after driving Alma's MG Midget into the viaduct at the end of *Coronation Street*?

12 Which Weatherfield villain died after being beaten up by Jim McDonald?

13 Who died from an overdose of sleeping pills when Ken Barlow refused to take her back?

14 Alma died from which disease: cancer, malaria or meningitis?

15 Sidney Templeton died on the back seat of whose car: Fred Elliott's, Mike Baldwin's or Roy Cropper's?

16 Which mild mannered *Coronation Street* resident died of a heart attack after being involved in a road rage incident?

17 Who was shot dead in a siege at Freshco's Supermarket?

18 Who froze to death, locked in a supermarket deep freeze after trying to blackmail Curly Watts?

19 Who died sat on a park bench watching Percy Sugden play bowls?

20 How was Maxine Peacock killed?

Answers on page 205

Mike Baldwin

1 Mike Baldwin came to Weatherfield from which city: Birmingham, Bristol or London?

2 How many times did Mike get married: three, four or five times?

3 Mike died in the arms of which great rival?

4 How many sons did Mike have?

5 What was Mike's middle name: Vernon, Vincent or Victor?

6 Mike was briefly married to which fellow textile factory owner?

7 What are the names of Mike's sons?

8 When Mike threw a party at the factory, which employee, thinking it was a fancy dress party turned up as Charlie Chaplin: Hilda Ogden, Ivy Tilsley or Ida Clough?

9 What was the name of the wine bar Mike opened with Alf Roberts and Len Fairclough?

10 Mike stepped in at the last minute to give away which *Coronation Street* bride: Gail, Vera or Ivy?

Answers on page 205

11 What was the name of the fancy clothes shop opened by Mike: The Western Front, The Eastern Front or The Southern Front?

12 Which of the following didn't Mike have a romance with: Dawn Prescott, Maggie Dunlop or Audrey Roberts?

13 Mike won whose taxi in a poker game: Steve McDonald's, Don Brennan's or Lloyd Mullaney's?

14 Which *Coronation Street* mechanic also acted as Mike's chauffeur: Kevin Webster, Brian Tilsley or Jim McDonald?

15 Which of Mike's wives seduced him by beating him at golf?

16 Mike went into partnership with which young underwear designer: Angie Freeman, Shirley Armitage or Gail Tilsley?

17 Which of Mike's wives also had an affair with his son Mark?

18 Towards the end of his life Baldwin suffered from what disease?

19 Both Mike's father and one of his former daughters-in-law shared the same name. What was it?

20 What is the name of the actor who played Mike Baldwin?

Answers on page 205

Ken Barlow

1 How many times has Ken Barlow been married: two, three or four times?

2 True or false: Ken was jailed for taking part in an anti Vietnam war demonstration?

3 What are the names of Ken's twins?

4 What was the name of Ken's first wife?

5 Who was Ken Barlow's arch nemesis?

6 What was Ken's second wife called: Jane, Janet or Janine?

7 Ken didn't have an affair with which of the following: Bet Lynch, Audrey Roberts or Alma Baldwin?

8 True or false: Tracy is not Ken's biological daughter?

9 What was Ken's footballer brother called: David, Darren or Douglas?

10 Which of the following jobs hasn't Ken had: supermarket trolley pusher, newspaper editor or lollipop man?

Answers on page 205

11 True or false: Ken once had a job as a male escort?

12 Ken and Deirdre first got married the day before which celebrated couple tied the knot?

13 Ken lived with which pensioner after the death of his first wife?

14 An affair with which woman ruined Ken's marriage with Deirdre?

15 How many girlfriends has Ken Barlow had: 17, 23 or 27?

16 Ken was arrested after punching which unruly pupil?

17 What is the name of Ken's grandson: Adam, Anthony or Alan?

18 Which hairdresser was the mother of Ken's son Daniel?

19 Ken's daughter Susan had a child with which Street rogue?

20 Ken and Deirdre remarried just before which Royal couple?

Answers on page 205

The Battersbys

1 What is the name of Les's adopted son?

2 Who was Leanne Battersby's first husband?

3 Leanne had an addiction to what: internet gambling, cocaine or vodka?

4 What household item did Les give to Janice as a wedding anniversary gift: an ironing board, a deep fat fryer or a vacuum cleaner?

5 What type of restaurant does Leanne own: Mexican, Italian or Spanish Tapas?

6 Janice left Les heartbroken after she had an affair with which family friend?

7 While Leanne was a prostitute she claimed to have what respectable job?

8 Which close friend of Toyah's went behind her back by sleeping with her boyfriend John Arnley?

9 Janice went to France with which Weatherfield plumber?

10 What is the name of Les's long lost son: Greg, Glen or Gary?

11 Janice had a street brawl with which fellow Underworld machinist after finding out about Leanne's prostitution?

12 Les went to prison after being framed for bashing whose new boyfriend: Leanne's, Toyah's or Janice's?

13 Leanne had an affair with which man while engaged to Jamie Baldwin?

14 Which group played at Les and Cilla's wedding reception?

15 Toyah had a relationship with which mechanic and stripper?

16 Which of Leanne's clients died crashing his car after he tried to kidnap her?

17 Cilla left Les to start a new life in which American city?

18 Why did Toyah pour de-icer into the deep freeze at Freshco?

19 Who stole Jack Duckworth's identity to become Leanne's business partner?

20 What happened to Les and Cilla when Schmeichel the dog jumped into the bath they were sharing?

Answers on page 205

The Duckworths

1 What is the name of Jack and Vera's rogue of a son?

2 Jack is a lover of which kind of animal: dogs, cats or pigeons?

3 What wedding anniversary did the Duckworths celebrate in 2007: silver, golden or ruby?

4 What home improvement did the Duckworths make to their house: loft conversion, stone cladding or a conservatory?

5 Who was Vera's best friend at Baldwin's Casuals: Ivy, Alma or Deirdre?

6 Jack and Vera married in which American city?

7 Jack had an affair with which Rovers barmaid: Bet Lynch, Liz McDonald or Gloria Todd?

8 What did Tyrone give to Jack for his 60th birthday?

9 The Duckworths sold number nine *Coronation Street* to which family in 1995?

10 Which one of the Duckworths took up nude modelling to earn some extra cash?

11 Which one of the following jobs hasn't Jack done: pall bearer, lollipop man or bin man?

12 Who hasn't lived with the Duckworths: Curly Watts, Tyrone Dobbs or Kevin Webster?

13 In addition to Jack, Vera also went out with which Rovers Return barman?

14 What are the names of the Duckworths' three grandchildren?

15 Why did Vera almost cause an international incident on a works jolly to France: she insulted the mayor, her knickers were hoisted up a flagpole or she was sick in a gendarme's helmet?

16 Which of the following places hasn't Vera worked at: supermarket, pub or bingo hall?

17 What was the name of the racehorse which Jack bought with Alf and Don: Three Lemons, Betty's Hotshot or Rovers Return?

18 Who tried to convince Vera that she was related to the Royal Family: Joss Shackleton, Mel Hutchwright or Victor Pendlebury?

19 What is the name of the actress who plays Vera?

20 What is the name of the actor who plays Jack?

Answers on page 206

The Grimshaws

1 Jason Grimshaw finally married which sweetheart at the second attempt?

2 What is Eileen Grimshaw's occupation?

3 Todd Grimshaw developed a fascination with which member of Sarah-Louise Platt's family?

4 Eileen had a relationship with which mechanic?

5 Which of the Grimshaws briefly left Weatherfield to work on the fairground in Blackpool?

6 Eileen went on holiday with Steve McDonald to which Mediterranean island: Malta, Corfu or Sicily?

7 Jason slept with his brother Todd's girlfriend. What was her name?

8 Todd had a relationship with which nurse?

9 Eileen inadvertently dated which convicted murderer?

10 True or false: Todd was *Coronation Street's* first openly gay character?

Answers on page 206

11 Jason dumped Violet after she kissed another man. Who did she snog?

12 True or false: Eileen was a singer in a band called The Bleak Industrial Blues Band?

13 At what number *Coronation Street* do the Grimshaws live: 11, 13 or 15?

14 Todd Grimshaw left Weatherfield to start a new life in which city?

15 What is Jason's occupation?

16 Who asked Eileen to join him travelling round Europe in Roy and Hayley's camper van?

17 Eileen and Gail Platt battled for the attention of which Weatherfield alternative therapist?

18 What is the name of the actor who plays Jason?

19 Eileen had a fling with which Streetcars driver?

20 Which Grimshaw was the father of Sarah-Louise's ill-fated baby Billy?

Answers on page 206

QUIZ 13 The McDonalds

1 Steve McDonald was married to which fiery brunette?

2 Liz McDonald was involved with which aging musician?

3 What was Jim McDonald's job prior to his arrival in Weatherfield: soldier, sailor or policeman?

4 Liz had a fling with which toyboy bookmaker: Colin Barnes, John Barnes or Peter Barnes?

5 What was the name of Steve's first wife?

6 True or false: Jim spent time in prison for burglary?

7 Which of the following hasn't Steve had an affair with: Maxine Heavey, Kelly Crabtree or Sally Webster?

8 Steve had a serious addiction to what: gambling, drinking or drugs?

9 Jim was imprisoned after beating up and killing which bad boy?

10 Liz gave birth to a daughter who died just one day old. What was her name: Katie, Kirsty or Kimberley?

11 Why did Steve spend two years in prison: perverting the course of justice, assault or drink driving?

Answers on page 206

12 Jim spent time in a wheelchair after suffering what type of accident: a car crash, a motorbike crash or a fall from scaffolding?

13 Liz had a steamy affair with which brewery delivery man?

14 Andy McDonald left Weatherfield to teach English in which country: Spain, Italy or Japan?

15 Liz briefly left Weatherfield to live in which seaside town: Blackpool, Morecambe or Southport?

16 Which of the following jobs hasn't Jim done: supermarket security guard, mechanic or plumber?

17 True or false: Liz ran off with Jim's physiotherapist, Michael Wall?

18 Jim had a spell as a chauffeur for which Weatherfield businessman: Mike Baldwin, Fred Elliott or Alec Gilroy?

19 Who was Steve's original business partner in the taxi firm Streetcars: Vikram Desai, Lloyd Mullaney or Les Battersby?

20 Steve had a relationship with a local gangster's estranged wife. What was her name?

Answers on page 206

The Platts

1 How many children does Gail have: two, three or four?

2 Who almost killed David by attempting to drown him in a bath tub?

3 Sarah-Louise stole husband Jason from which Rovers barmaid?

4 What was Gail's maiden name?

5 Martin had an ill-fated relationship with which 16 year old?

6 How old was Sarah when she became pregnant with her first child: 13, 14 or 15?

7 How many husbands has Gail had?

8 How did Craig Harris try and kill Martin: he messed with the brakes on his car, he tried to poison him or tried to push him from a roof?

9 Gail was propositioned by a man who shares a name with which Olympic Champion: Colin Jackson, Allan Wells or Roger Bannister?

10 How did David try and kill Jason Grimshaw: he tried to run him over, he shot him or he loosened the bolts on some scaffolding causing a fall?

11 Sarah was almost killed after going joyriding with which naughty schoolboy?

12 Gail's son Nicky left *Coronation Street* for which country: America, Australia or Canada?

13 Who sent cards signed by Richard to Gail and was later revealed as the Hillman Hoaxer?

14 What is the name of Sarah's daughter?

15 Martin left Weatherfield to start a new life in which northern city: Leeds, Liverpool or Newcastle?

16 What happened to Sarah's wedding dress: it was burnt on Bonfire Night, it shrank in the wash or it got covered in oil?

17 Gail had a relationship with which reflexologist from the Medical Centre?

18 What was the name of Sarah and Todd Grimshaw's baby who died just two days old?

19 What is the name of the actress who plays Sarah?

20 What is the name of the actress who plays Gail?

Answers on page 206

Rovers Return

1 Who took over as landlady of the Rovers after Fred Elliott sold up?

2 Which of the following hasn't at one time been owner of the Rovers: Jack Duckworth, Ken Barlow or Mike Baldwin?

3 What type of food does the Rovers specialise in: hot pot, shepherd's pie or bangers and mash?

4 The Rovers Return was originally owned by which brewery?

5 The Rovers occupies the corner of Coronation and which other street: Rosamund Street, Market Street or Curzon Street?

6 What was the name of Annie Walker's husband: Jack, Jim or Jerry?

7 Which character celebrated 30 years of working at the Rovers in 1999?

8 What was the name of Annie Walker's son who took over at the Rovers when she retired?

9 True or false: the Rovers Return contains a dartboard?

10 What was the name of the bar next to the Rovers which was run by Alec Gilroy: The Graffiti Club, Byron's or Bar Nevada?

Answers on page 206

11 Which of the following isn't a rival pub to the Rovers: The Flying Horse, The Weatherfield Arms or The Golden Lion?

12 When the Rovers caught fire in 1986 which moustachioed mechanic rescued Bet Lynch?

13 Which former rugby league player briefly owned the Rovers?

14 Who took over the Rovers after Bet's departure?

15 What was the name of Alec Gilroy's granddaughter who moved in with him at the Rovers: Vicky, Tracy or Sandra?

16 Which manageress from the Rovers suffered a nervous breakdown after her ill treatment at the hands of Charlie Stubbs?

17 Which Rovers potman dated Liz McDonald and was in a band called The Rhythm Rascals?

18 The husband of which Rovers landlady was murdered by thugs looking for her son?

19 True or false: Emily Bishop used to work behind the bar at the Rovers?

20 Duggie Ferguson originally bought the Rovers with which two Weatherfield businessmen?

Answers on page 206

Doctors

1 What is the name of the surgery in *Doctors*?

2 *Doctors* is set in which fictional suburb: Lacebridge, Letherbridge or Denimbridge?

3 Who was left paralysed after Dr George Woodson crashed her car into a skip?

4 Greg's partner Rico is from which country: Spain, Brazil or Argentina?

5 What is the name of George Woodson's baby?

6 Nigel tried to blackmail Melody after he found out she spent ages doing what at work: playing internet poker, buying shoes online or using dating sites?

7 Dr Jimmi Clay suffers from which condition: agoraphobia, obsessive-compulsive disorder or vertigo?

8 Who discovered that she was having a relationship with her half-brother?

9 What is Ronnie Woodson's profession: solicitor, doctor or detective?

10 Why was Donna sacked from the surgery: breaking patient confidentiality, drinking at work or having an affair with a patient?

Answers on page 207

11 Where did Elizabeth reveal to Nick that she had had an abortion: at Greg's wedding, on holiday or in the surgery waiting room?

12 What is the name of the surgery's receptionist: Vivien March, Vivien May or Vivien June?

13 Which actor played Dr Brendan 'Mac' McGuire, the founder of the surgery?

14 Why was Greg suspended from duty: he had an affair with a patient, drinking on the job or giving a potassium chloride injection instead of insulin?

15 Whose marriage lasted just six weeks after she found her sister in bed with her husband?

16 Who tried to kill Nick, suspending him from a cliff while rock climbing?

17 Which doctor was charged with assault after disturbing a burglar?

18 George missed out on meeting which Royal after a row with Susie: The Queen, Prince Charles or Prince William?

19 Who was held at gunpoint by a distressed Alex at the barn?

20 Which doctor joined the surgery after being a major in the Royal Army Medical Corps: Dr Marc Eliot, Dr Greg Robinson or Dr Joe Fenton?

Answers on page 207

EastEnders
The Early Years

QUIZ 17

1 What was the name of Pete and Pauline's brother: Kenny, Kevin or Keith?

2 Who was found dying in his flat in the first ever episode of *EastEnders*?

3 Andy O'Brien had what occupation?

4 Who were the first gay couple to appear in Albert Square?

5 Pete Beale was a big fan of what type of music?

6 Lofty Holloway tried and failed to get what job: policeman, fireman or traffic warden?

7 Who gambled his entire business in a game of poker?

8 Benny Bloom was the boyfriend of which elderly Albert Square resident?

9 Who won Miss Walford 1986: Sharon, Cindy or Michelle?

10 How did Sue and Ali Osman's baby die?

11 Who was Kathy Beale's drug addict daughter: Donna, Debbie or Deirdre?

12 What was the name of Ali Osman's brother?

13 What was Rod Norman's nickname: Rod the rapper, Rod the roadie or Rod the rascal?

14 Who briefly found religion in the shape of a vicar called Duncan?

15 Den and Angie went on an ill-fated second honeymoon to which romantic city: Rome, Paris or Venice?

16 What was the name of the brewery rep who was bribed by Pat and Frank: Magpie, Budgie or Sparrow?

17 Nick Cotton persuaded which young homeless girl to become a prostitute: Mary, Martha or Marian Smith?

18 Which family were the owners of the First Til Last Shop: The Kapurs, The Kumars or The Karims?

19 Who appeared in a fictional TV gameshow called *Cat and Mouse*: Michelle Fowler, Pauline Fowler or Arthur Fowler?

20 Julie Cooper ran what Albert Square establishment: hairdressers, market stall or bookmakers?

Answers on page 207

EastEnders The 1990s

1 Which heartbroken Walford resident unsuccessfully tried to kill himself by crashing his van?

2 Which pair of young lovers eloped and married in Gretna Green?

3 Who left Hattie Tavernier just days before they were due to be married?

4 Which landlord of the Queen Vic used to be a policeman?

5 Grant Mitchell ended his relationship with Nina after he found out she used to do what for a living?

6 What was Richard Cole better known as?

7 Who was the elderly lady who lodged with the Fowlers: Auntie Betty, Auntie Nelly or Auntie Jeany?

8 Steve Owen accidentally killed which former girlfriend?

9 Who was the young Irish footballer who played for Walford Town FC and lodged with the Fowlers: Jimmy Flood, Aidan Brosnan or Liam Doyle?

10 Which member of the Mitchell clan beat up Eddie Royle so badly that he needed brain surgery: Grant, Phil or Billy?

Answers on page 207

11 Who ran away from home and ended up sleeping rough for three months: Bianca Jackson, Diane Butcher or Martin Fowler?

12 Which member of the di Marco family was a police officer: Beppe, Gianni or Teresa?

13 What was the name of Sanjay Kapoor's wife?

14 What was Richard Cole's job: market inspector, traffic warden or takeaway owner?

15 Who did Nigel Bates marry in 1994: Donna, Debbie or Denise?

16 Mark Fowler and his wife Ruth split after she had an affair with which Irish charmer?

17 Barry was conned out of £140,000 by which schemer: Vanessa Carlton, Victoria Carlton or Veronica Carlton?

18 Joe, the long lost son of which Albert Square resident arrived in Walford in 1996?

19 Pauline Fowler had a brief platonic relationship with which singer: Danny Taurus, Danny Gemini or Danny Libra?

20 Who kidnapped Tiffany Mitchell's baby Courtney and threatened to throw her off a cliff?

Answers on page 207

QUIZ 19
EastEnders
The Modern Era

1 Stacey Slater had an affair with which older man?

2 Who did Martin Fowler kidnap and hold for ransom?

3 Libby Fox and Darren Miller started a computer business by pretending to be which person: Li Chong, Stacey Slater or Kevin Wicks?

4 What bombshell did Kevin Wicks drop on Deano and Carly?

5 Which pair had a cat fight in the Queen Vic at Peggy Mitchell's 65th birthday party?

6 Bradley once greeted Stacey wearing just what to cover his modesty: a champagne bottle and a bow tie, a fig leaf or a leopardskin thong?

7 Who proposed to Dawn Swann on a day trip to Brighton?

8 True or false: Stella Crawford found a pig in her bedroom?

9 Who kidnapped Ian Beale?

10 What was the name of the French exchange student who stayed with the Beales: Monique, Yvette or Edith?

11 Which pregnant woman was rushed to hospital after Jase Dyer's old crew trashed the Queen Vic?

12 Ronnie and Roxy Mitchell arrived in Walford from which island?

13 Who did Phil Mitchell get to smash up Kevin Wicks's cars?

14 Garry Hobbs went on an 18-30 holiday to which party island: Tenerife, Lanzarote or Corfu?

15 Which character said 'you may not have done it before but I've done it loads' before a night of passion?

16 Who had a market stall called Urban Alternative?

17 What is the name of Tanya Branning's drug addict sister?

18 Which pair tried to frame Sean for the attack on Patrick Trueman?

19 Why did Bradley have to delay proposing to Stacey: he'd lost the ring, he triggered his nut allergy or he'd lost his voice?

20 What smashed the window to Ian Beale's fish and chip shop?

Answers on page 207

Around Walford

QUIZ 20

1 What is the name of the square in Walford: Elizabeth Square, Victoria Square or Albert Square?

2 On what street in Walford is the market located?

3 Wilmott-Brown was the landlord of which Walford pub?

4 What was the name of the taxi firm run by Ali and Mehmet?

5 What is the postcode of the Walford area: E17, E19 or E20?

6 The bench in the garden in the centre of the Square is named after which ill-fated character?

7 Where would you find Mitchell's Autos?

8 Scarlet's Nightclub is named after the daughter of which character?

9 What was the name of the second-hand car lot owned by Pat, Ricky Butcher and David Wicks?

10 Who is the lesser spotted owner of the launderette?

Answers on page 207

11 What was the name of the dating agency run by Natalie Evans: Romantic Relations, Love's Young Dream or Wedded Bliss?

12 The cafe on Bridge Street is named after which character?

13 What is the name of Walford's fish and chip shop?

14 Sophisti-Kate was what type of business: hairdressers, clothes shop or a nail bar?

15 What was the name of the restaurant run by the di Marco family?

16 Who were the owners of F&P Cabs?

17 What is the name of Walford's leading Indian restaurant: Argee Bhajee, Ruby's or Mirch Masala?

18 Who became the owner of Walford's bookies after the death of Dennis Watts?

19 What was the name of the catering company run by Ian Beale and Hattie Tavernier?

20 What is the name of the tube station in Walford: Walford South, Walford East or Walford West?

Answers on page 207

Ian Beale

1 What are the names of Ian Beale's parents?

2 How many times has Ian been married: two, three or four times?

3 What are the names of Ian's two biological sons?

4 Ian has a much younger half-brother. What is his name?

5 What is the name of Ian's only daughter?

6 Who was Ian's second wife?

7 Why did she leave him?

8 What was the name of the nanny who Ian later married?

9 True or false: Ian appeared in the first ever episode of *EastEnders*?

10 Where did Ian meet Jane Collins: at the fair, in the pub or at the chip shop?

11 Cindy Beale had a child with which close friend of Ian's?

12 True or false: Ian Beale was voted as one of the top five TV characters we love to hate in a 2001 poll?

13 What is the name of Ian's fish and chip shop?

14 Ian made regular visits to which Walford prostitute?

15 How did Ian's wife Laura die?

16 Who hired a hit man to try and kill Ian: Cindy, Mel or Steven?

17 What is Ian Beale's middle name: Albert, Edward or George?

18 Ian tried to have which dog killed after it bit him on the bum: Roly, Wellard or Terrence?

19 Ian's wife Jane slept with which member of the Mitchell family: Phil, Grant or Billy?

20 What is the name of the actor who plays Ian Beale?

Answers on page 208

Dot and Jim Branning

1 What was the name of Dot's first husband?

2 Dot works in which Albert Square establishment?

3 On what day of the year did Dot and Jim get married: St Valentine's Day, Christmas Day or Boxing Day?

4 Dot helped which elderly friend to die in a euthanasia pact?

5 What is the name of Dot's bad boy son?

6 True or false: Dot appeared in the first ever episode of *EastEnders*?

7 Which Albert Square establishment does Jim work in?

8 Which of Jim's daughters was married to Alan: Karen, Carol or Carly?

9 What was the name of Dot's grandson: Ashley, Adam or Anthony?

10 Who was the lodger who briefly lived with Dot: Nigel, Norman or Neville?

11 Dot served a spell in prison for which offence: shoplifting, fraud or drunk and disorderly?

12 Dot's son tried to poison her to gain what: her house, her bingo winnings or her car?

13 Which of Jim's grandchildren was originally arrested for the murder of Pauline Fowler?

14 Dot's grandson died riding whose motorbike: Mark Fowler's, Martin Fowler's or Ian Beale's?

15 What is the name of Jim's great granddaughter: Rebecca, Rachel or Ruby?

16 True or false: there is a gay club night in Cambridge called the Dot Cotton Club?

17 Dot was beaten and robbed by what type of conman: fake charity collector, fake plumber or fake builder?

18 What was the name of the baby who Dot and Jim found abandoned in a Kent church: Tomas, Taylor or Timothy?

19 What is the name of the actress who plays Dot?

20 What is the name of the actor who plays Jim?

Answers on page 208

Pat Butcher

1 What was the name of Pat's first husband?

2 What are the names of Pat's two sons?

3 Pat is the manageress of which Walford gambling emporium: a bookmakers, a dog track or a casino?

4 True or false: Pat once ran the B&B?

5 Which of the following hasn't Pat had a fling with: Patrick Trueman, Charlie Slater or Den Watts?

6 Pat married which wheeler dealer in 1989?

7 What was the name of Pat's stepdaughter from hell: Janice, Janine or Jenny?

8 Pat was imprisoned for what offence: drink driving, fraud or soliciting?

9 What is the name of Pat's grandson who returned from New Zealand in 2007: Stephen, Simon or Shaun?

10 What was the name of the taxi firm which Pat opened: PatCabs, Butcher's Cars or PB Chauffeurs?

11 Pat inherited the house of which EastEnd bad boy after his untimely death?

Answers on page 208

12 Who slapped Pat in the Queen Vic after finding out about her affair with Frank?

13 Which dependable used car dealer became Pat's fourth husband?

14 Who evicted Pat from the family home after the death of her fourth husband: Grant Mitchell, Ian Beale or Barry Evans?

15 True or false: in her early days in the Square Pat was a prostitute?

16 When hit by financial problems, Pat was caught stealing from whose purse: Peggy, Sharon or Cindy?

17 Which of Pat's husbands almost died after taking black market viagra?

18 What was the name of Pat's sister who spent most of her life in a mental institution: Jean, Joan or June?

19 What was Pat's maiden name: Smith, Harris or Johnson?

20 What is the name of the actress who plays Pat: Pam St Clement, Gillian Taylforth or Wendy Richard?

Answers on page 208

The Queen Vic

1 Who famously handed divorce papers to his wife in the Queen Vic on Christmas Day 1986?

2 What colour is the exterior of the Queen Vic: red, blue or brown?

3 Which Queen Vic manager got married in the pub on Christmas Day 2003?

4 Which of the following hasn't been landlord of the Queen Vic: Dan Sullivan, Eddie Royle or Pete Beale?

5 Which of the following hasn't been a landlady of the Queen Vic: Pauline Fowler, Pat Butcher or Sharon Watts?

6 Who has been a barmaid, landlady and manageress of the Queen Vic and also been barred from the pub?

7 Who fell down the stairs of the Queen Vic, accusing her husband of pushing her?

8 Who set fire to the Queen Vic in an insurance fiddle on Sharon's birthday in 1992?

9 Who was murdered in the Queen Vic in 2005?

10 Which Queen Vic landlord was murdered by Nick Cotton?

11 What was the name of Den's very posh mistress: Jan, Jen or June?

12 What was the name of the yuppie pub which was the rival to the Queen Vic?

13 Which nasty piece of work was its landlord?

14 What is the name of the Queen Vic's work-shy potman: Jim Branning, Patrick Trueman or Billy Mitchell?

15 Who sold his share of the Queen Vic to Dan Sullivan for just £5: Phil Mitchell, Grant Mitchell or Frank Butcher?

16 Which character conceived both of her children in the bar of the Queen Vic?

17 Den Watts was murdered in the Queen Vic by what implement: a knife, a poker or a dog-shaped doorstop?

18 What is the name of the long-serving barmaid who rarely speaks a line: Tracy, Diana or Shirley?

19 Who tried to sell the Queen Vic to Ian Beale after forging Den's signature on the transfer deed?

20 Peggy Mitchell smashed up the Queen Vic after finding out about the terrible behaviour of which lover?

Answers on page 208

The Fowlers

QUIZ 25

1 Who was the father of Michelle Fowler's first child Vicki?

2 How old was Michelle when she first got pregnant: 16, 17 or 18?

3 Michelle was married to which short-sighted softie?

4 Mark Fowler ran which stall at the market?

5 Which Albert Square bad boy gave Martin dodgy ecstasy tablets?

6 Vicki arrived in Albert Square after previously living in which country: USA, Australia or South Africa?

7 Martin Fowler went to prison after knocking over and killing which Albert Square youngster?

8 Pauline met her second husband at what unlikely venue: a bridge club, a casino or at a salsa dancing class?

9 What was the name of Mark's Scottish wife?

10 Michelle almost got married to which university lecturer: Geoff Barnes, Cliff Barnes or John Barnes?

11 Arthur Fowler was imprisoned for embezzlement after being framed by which supposed old friend: Willy Roper, Charlie Cotton or Nigel Bates?

12 Who is the unlikely father of Michelle's second child, Mark Junior?

13 Arthur had an affair with which lonely divorcee?

14 Mark suffered from which disease: HIV, cancer or MS?

15 Vicki had an abortion after sleeping with whom: Spencer Moon, Alfie Moon or Ash Ferreira?

16 What was the name of Mark's third wife: Laura, Lisa or Lorraine?

17 Pauline turned down which odd job man's proposal of marriage?

18 Martin Fowler was stalked by which mentally unstable barmaid?

19 Actor James Alexandrou played which member of the Fowler clan?

20 Mark's first wife died just a day after they were married. What was her name: Gill, Gail or Glenda?

Answers on page 208

The Mitchells

QUIZ 26

1 What are the names of Peggy Mitchell's three children?

2 Peggy was briefly engaged to which member of the Slater family?

3 What was the name of the policewoman who investigated Phil and ended up marrying him?

4 Grant Mitchell served in which branch of the armed forces: the Paras, the Marines or the SAS?

5 What was the name of Peggy's dodgy gangster boyfriend?

6 Who is the mother of Phil Mitchell's son Ben?

7 Who did Peggy marry in 1999?

8 Sam Mitchell has been married twice. Who were her two husbands?

9 Jamie Mitchell was killed after being hit by a car driven by which distracted driver?

10 What is the name of Grant's daughter with Tiffany?

Answers on page 209

11 Which Mitchell started the fire at Angie's Den: Grant, Phil or Billy?

12 Who shot Phil Mitchell?

13 What is the name of Grant's Brazilian wife: Carla, Carmen or Carmel?

14 Sam Mitchell had a fling with which of the di Marco brothers?

15 Phil Mitchell was involved in a marriage of convenience with which Romanian refugee?

16 Which Mitchell is the father of Mark Fowler Junior?

17 What are the names of Peggy's nieces who moved into the Queen Vic in 2007?

18 Phil had an affair with which fellow Alcoholics Anonymous attendee?

19 Which Mitchell was responsible for torching Frank's car lot in an insurance scam, killing a homeless boy in the process?

20 Grant had an affair with the mother of one of his wives. What was her name?

Answers on page 209

The Slaters

1 What is Charlie Slater's occupation?

2 What was the name of Charlie's horrible brother?

3 Dr Trueman was engaged to which of the Slater sisters?

4 Mo ended up delivering whose unexpected baby?

5 In which unique way did Billy Mitchell propose to Little Mo Slater?

6 Who was hit in the bum by a mis-aimed dart in a game at the Queen Vic: Mo, Charlie or Sean?

7 Where did Kat and Alfie get married: a church, a registry office or at the Queen Vic?

8 Why did Charlie serve time in prison: drink driving, dangerous driving or he beat someone up?

9 What is the name of Sean and Stacey's mum: June, Joan or Jean?

10 Kat Slater had a relationship with which Albert Square doctor?

Answers on page 209

11 Little Mo almost killed Trevor after hitting him with which household object: kettle, iron or vacuum cleaner?

12 Which of the Slater sisters married Garry Hobbs?

13 Mo had a relationship with which northern wide-boy?

14 Which of the following hasn't Sean Slater had a relationship with: Carly Wicks, Preeti Choraria or Dawn Swan?

15 Which Slater was involved in the murder of Den Watts?

16 What is the name of the lesser spotted Slater sister who usually lives in Lanzarote: Belinda, Beverly or Bernice?

17 Kat slept with which Walford wide boy to pay off a debt incurred by husband Alfie?

18 Who once set up a sex chatline and called herself Madame Whiplash: Mo, Little Mo or Kat?

19 Little Mo had a relationship with which Walford doctor?

20 Who did Stacey try to blackmail after they had slept together?

Answers on page 209

Sharon Watts

1 Sharon was married to which member of the Mitchell family?

2 Sharon has one half-brother and one half-sister. What are their names?

3 What was the name of the group which Sharon formed with Kelvin Carpenter: The Banned, The Strand or The Canned?

4 True or false: Den and Angie were Sharon's biological parents?

5 What did Den often call Sharon: Princess, Sweet Pea or Darling?

6 Despite being supposedly infertile, Sharon had a baby with which man?

7 How did Grant find out that Sharon had cheated on him with Phil: on a baby intercom, via a text message or on a cassette tape?

8 What name did Sharon give to the E20 club after she took it over?

9 Sharon had her heart broken after the death of which fireman?

10 True or false: Sharon had an affair with Billy Mitchell?

Answers on page 209

11 What was the unlikely profession of Duncan Boyd who Sharon was briefly engaged to: a vicar, a librarian or a vet?

12 Sharon fled Walford to start a new life in which country: Australia, America or Brazil?

13 Where did Sharon and Phil tie the knot: in a church, in a register office or at the Queen Vic?

14 Sharon's fireman boyfriend died while trying to rescue which Albert Square villain?

15 Wicksy played away behind Sharon's back with which scheming blonde?

16 True or false: Den's dead body was found on Sharon and Dennis's wedding day?

17 Sharon was trapped after who set fire to the Queen Vic in an insurance scam?

18 Who killed Sharon's husband Dennis: Spencer Moon, Alfie Moon or Danny Moon?

19 Sharon's affair with Phil was revealed at whose engagement party?

20 What is the name of the actress who plays Sharon?

Answers on page 209

EastEnders Deaths

1 Who died after being struck by a dog-shaped doorstop?

2 Tiffany Mitchell died after being struck by a car driven by which driver?

3 Who murdered Eddie Royle?

4 How did Barry Evans die?

5 How did young Hassan Osman die?

6 Martin Fowler knocked over and killed which member of the Mitchell clan?

7 Who died in the first episode of *EastEnders*?

8 Steve Owen died after a car chase involving which of the Mitchells?

9 How did Pauline Fowler's second husband Joe Macer die?

10 Which Walford wide boy died after being pushed off a flyover?

Answers on page 209

11 Who fell down the stairs and died after slipping on a toy: Laura Beale, Kathy Beale or Pete Beale?

12 Saskia Duncan was killed by what implement: an ash tray, a stapler or pint glass?

13 Who died while trying to rescue Trevor Morgan from a fire at the Slater house?

14 Who killed Dennis Rickman?

15 Ashley Cotton died while riding whose motorbike?

16 How did both Arthur and Pauline Fowler die: brain haemorrhage, heart attack or cancer?

17 Who, with the help of her best friend, died on her 86th birthday?

18 Which Walford vixen died in prison while giving birth to her fourth child?

19 How did Stella Crawford kill herself?

20 True or false: Roy Evans died in a car crash?

Answers on page 209

Emmerdale The 1970s

1 In what year did *Emmerdale* first appear on TV screens: 1971, 1972 or 1973?

2 The first episode of *Emmerdale* centred around which event: a christening, a wedding or a funeral?

3 True or false: *Emmerdale Farm* was originally only broadcast in the Yorkshire region?

4 Who was raped and murdered by the evil Jim Latimer?

5 What was the name of the local Squire of the Manor: George Verney, George Burley or George Melly?

6 True or false: Mr Wilks's daughter was called Martha?

7 What was Seth Armstrong's occupation before become a gamekeeper: barman, school caretaker or milkman?

8 Who was the first woman to be employed by Amos and Mr Wilks at The Woolpack: Dolly, Polly or Molly?

9 What were the names of Matt Skilbeck's young twins?

10 Steve Hawker and Pip Coulter were involved in an armed robbery at which establishment: The Woolpack, Home Farm or the Post Office?

Answers on page 209

11 What was the name of the tramp who died after falling from a window at The Old Mill?

12 Bad boy Phil Fletcher was accidentally shot by which member of the Sugden family?

13 Edward Ruskin, William Hockley, David Cowper and Donald Hinton all held what position in the village?

14 Who gave birth to twins but died of a brain haemorrhage shortly afterwards?

15 What was the name of Joe Sugden's first wife: Christine, Charlotte or Catherine?

16 Which man who was normally found in The Woolpack became a reporter for the *Hotten Courier*?

17 What was the name of Seth Armstrong's son: John, Jimmy or Josiah?

18 Why was the original Woolpack forced to close: subsidence, a dangerous chimney or a broken roof?

19 True or false: the company which took over Home Farm was called LA Estates.

20 Gwyneth Powell who played Julie Croft, is best known for playing which school headmistress?

Answers on page 209

Emmerdale The 1980s

1 Jack Sugden returned to the village after living in which city: Rome, Paris or Berlin?

2 What was the name of Matt Skilbeck's second wife?

3 Who was Kathy Bates's first husband?

4 Which mischievous, Bible bashing neighbour of the Sugdens died when his tractor overturned?

5 Where did Jack Sugden meet future wife Sarah: at Home Farm, at The Woolpack or at the mobile library?

6 Who surprisingly became addicted to a Space Invaders machine?

7 The Woolpack had a healthy rivalry with which local pub: The Malt Shovel, The Masons Arms or The Golden Lion?

8 What was the name of Seth Armstrong's long-suffering first wife?

9 Ruth Pennington had an affair with Joe Sugden. What was her occupation?

10 Who knocked over Jackie Merrick in an horrific motorcycle accident?

11 Who tried to run away from home to live with his dad in Germany but only made it to Hull?

12 Jack Sugden had an affair with Karen Moore. What was her occupation?

13 Why was Seth barred from The Woolpack after a visit from the Bishop of Hotten?

14 There was outrage in the village at plans to build what?

15 Who fell down a mineshaft while trying to rescue a sheep: Jack Sugden, Joe Sugden or Jackie Merrick?

16 Which teenager got pregnant by Andy Longthorne?

17 Who foiled a raid at the Post Office but kept some of the cash which the thieves left behind?

18 Which actor, better known for his time in *EastEnders*, played Graham Lodsworth?

19 True or false: Kathy miscarried after catching a disease from a sheep?

20 Who in 1989 bought Home Farm?

Emmerdale The 1990s

1 Amos Brearly left The Woolpack and retired to which country?

2 Kim Tate had an affair with which Right Honourable Master Of The Hounds?

3 What was the name of Eric Pollard's Filipino bride?

4 Who in 1999 became the first landlady of The Woolpack?

5 Zoe Tate had a relationship with Emma Nightingale. What was Emma's occupation?

6 What was the name of the village's crooked councillor: Charlie Aindow, Bert Bradshaw or Arthur Rose?

7 Who was jailed for shooting a poacher?

8 Kelly Windsor married which member of the Glover family?

9 When Frank Tate lay dying of a heart attack what did his wife Kim do: called an ambulance, gave him the kiss of life or touched up her lipstick?

10 True or false: Kathy took HGV driving lessons?

11 Which cricket legend appeared in *Emmerdale* to re-open
The Woolpack: Geoffrey Boycott, Ian Botham or Fred Trueman?

12 What was the name of the hamburger stall run by Mandy
Dingle: McDingles, The Munch Box or The Fatty Eater?

13 Who got engaged to Eric Pollard then ran off with £2,000
he'd giver her to open an antique shop?

14 The wife of which Woolpack landlord was shot and killed
in a raid on the Post Office?

15 Who had an affair with wine merchant Josh Lewis?

16 Which 13-year-old gave birth to a child called Geri?

17 Viv Windsor had an affair with which Woolpack barman?

18 Who was sent to prison for manslaughter after running
over Pete Whiteley?

19 How did Steve Marchant try and kill Eric Pollard: tampered
with his brakes, poisoned him or shot him?

20 Which villager briefly found love with a biker called
Jo Steadman?

Answers on page 210

Emmerdale Modern Day

1 What are the names of Viv and Bob Hope's twins?

2 Policeman Ross is the cousin of which long term *Emmerdale* resident?

3 Alice Dingle suffered from what disease?

4 Diane Lambert cheated on Jack with which former prisoner?

5 Where did Viv Hope give birth to the twins?

6 Who delivered the twins?

7 Terry Woods spotted his dad Duke on which real life TV talk show?

8 Emily Kirk left *Emmerdale* to take up what profession?

9 Which barmaid left the village after realising that Paddy's proposal of marriage happened by accident?

10 Who died of a heart attack while celebrating the village's 500th anniversary?

11 Sharon Lambert was engaged to which footballer?

Answers on page 210

12 Louise Appleton had a fling with which *Emmerdale* toyboy?

13 Jo Stiles rescued what type of animal from certain death: a goat, a sheep or a pig?

14 Who in 2007 poured petrol throughout Annie's Cottage which led to the terrible fire?

15 Which drunken Dingle crashed Debbie's cab?

16 How was Pearl Ladderbanks scammed: an internet get rich quick scheme, a rogue trader or by a charity collector?

17 Who ordered Eli to tamper with the brakes on Billy's truck which led to a crash?

18 Which Swedish pop group recorded an album called *Emmerdale*?

19 Grace Barraclough had an ill-advised affair with which *Emmerdale* resident: Cain Dingle, Carl King or Bob Hope?

20 Who set fire to the back room of The Woolpack with a discarded cigarette?

Answers on page 210

Emmerdale Deaths

1 Who was crushed to death by a fallen chimney in the great storm of 2003?

2 Leonard Kampinksi, Archie Brooks, Elizabeth Pollard and Mark Hughes all died in what disaster?

3 The first ever episode of *Emmerdale* featured the funeral of which character: Jacob Sugden, James Sugden or Julian Sugden?

4 Which *Emmerdale* businessman died from a heart attack after the return of his supposedly dead wife?

5 How did Sarah Sugden die: in a car crash, in a fire or by drowning?

6 Who shot Liam Hammond: Frank Tate, Zoe Tate or Chris Tate?

7 Which Dingle died in a bus crash: Sam, Butch or Cain?

8 Who died in a fire while trying to rescue Kim Tate's young baby James?

9 Chris Tate committed suicide but who did he try to frame for murder?

10 How did Ray Mullen die?

Answers on page 210

11 Who allegedly murdered his wife but wasn't discovered because of the plane crash?

12 Which police officer died in 2007 after being hit by a lorry?

13 Vic Windsor was shot dead by which armed robber?

14 Rachel Hughes was killed by which *Emmerdale* schoolteacher?

15 Which *Emmerdale* police officer died in a car crash while in pursuit of Cain Dingle?

16 Linda Fowler died in a car crash after the driver, Alex Oakwell tried to do what: snort cocaine, drink some whisky or change his tie?

17 Who died after his car went over a cliff and burst into flames?

18 True or false: Dodgy businessman Dennis Rigg was gored to death by a bull?

19 Who helped Alice Dingle to die by giving her an overdose of morphine?

20 Which three characters died in the King show home explosion?

Answers on page 210

Around Emmerdale

1 *Emmerdale* is set in which English county: Lancashire, Northumbria or Yorkshire?

2 What is the name of *Emmerdale's* pub?

3 Which family live at Wishing Well Cottage?

4 What was the original name of the village of *Emmerdale*: Beckingale, Beckinsale or Beckindale?

5 Who converted The Old School House into the Old School Tea Rooms after receiving money from a divorce settlement?

6 What is the name of the cottage which Edna Birch lives in: Woodbine, Woodurn or Woodsmoke?

7 The hill overlooking *Emmerdale* was renamed after which character who was killed in the *Emmerdale* plane crash?

8 What is the name of the church in *Emmerdale*?

9 Smithy Cottage is the home to what business?

10 What is the name of *Emmerdale's* Bed and Breakfast?

Answers on page 210

11 Betty Eagleton lives at which cottage: Keeper's Cottage, Sleeper's Cottage or Sweeper's Cottage?

12 Which wine bar owner lost his licence for selling alcohol to underage drinkers?

13 What was the name of the cottage bought by Tom King for the headquarters of King and Sons: Apple Tree Cottage, Pear Tree Cottage or Peach Cottage?

14 What was the name of the restaurant which replaced Kathy's Diner?

15 Which character died after falling from scaffolding at the King's Holdgate Farm?

16 Which family bought Home Farm from NY Estates?

17 What is the name of the nearest major town to *Emmerdale*: Totten, Hotten or Rotten?

18 Who took over the running of the Garage from Lisa Dingle?

19 Which family bought the Post Office in 1993?

20 Who set up the Dale Park Holiday Village: Eric Pollard, Tom King or Frank Tate?

Answers on page 210

QUIZ 36 The Dingles

1 What is the name of Zak and Lisa Dingle's young daughter: Belle, Bonny or Betty?

2 Cain Dingle had a fling with which *Emmerdale* policewoman?

3 *Emmerdale* vet Paddy Kirk was married to which Dingle: Tina, Mandy or Charity?

4 Which Dingle made her *Emmerdale* debut at Marlon's stag do as a stripogram dressed as a nun?

5 What is Sam Dingle's son called?

6 Who are Debbie Dingle's real parents?

7 Which Dingle once dyed Eric Pollard's moustache pink?

8 How are Eli and Marlon Dingle related: nephew and uncle, brothers or cousins?

9 Who woke up next to a dead body after bedding gangster Colin McFarlane?

10 Which of the following isn't the name of one of Zak's brothers: Shadrach, Ezra, Caleb or Josiah?

11 How did Butch Dingle die?

Answers on page 211

12 What is the name of the Dingle family home?

13 Zak Dingle was diagnosed with what type of cancer: skin, liver or testicular?

14 Which Dingle did Eli accidentally shoot during a botched armed robbery?

15 Sam Dingle knocked over and almost killed which *Emmerdale* pensioner?

16 Which Dingle had a lesbian fling with Zoe Tate: Charity, Chastity or Tina?

17 Zak's first appearance in *Emmerdale* saw him having a punch up with which character: Ned Glover, Chris Tate or Frank Tate?

18 Charity Dingle had a one-night stand with which married cousin?

19 What was the name of Lisa Dingle's ex-husband who tried to blow up the Dingle home: Barry, Bernie or Barney?

20 Which of the following isn't a member of the extended Dingle clan: Brando Dingle, Albert Ezekiel Dingle or Tom Cruise Dingle?

Answers on page 211

The Kings

QUIZ 37

1 Who is the eldest of the King brothers: Jimmy, Carl or Matthew?

2 Carl King was engaged to which member of the Dingle family: Charity, Chastity or Tina?

3 What was Max King's occupation: vet, doctor or lawyer?

4 Tom King was engaged to which Dingle: Charity, Chastity or Tina?

5 What was the name of Carl King's estranged wife: Colleen, Carmen or Christine?

6 Who is Tom King's illegitimate daughter?

7 Carl accidentally caused the death of Paul Marsden. What was Marsden's occupation: postman, binman or milkman?

8 How did Paul Marsden die?

9 What are the names of Carl's two children?

10 Which King botched a repair job which led to a deadly gas explosion at the show home?

Answers on page 211

11 Jimmy jilted which *Emmerdale* vixen after finding out that she'd snogged Eli Dingle?

12 Who slapped Carl after finding out that he was married?

13 Jimmy King was married to which blonde bombshell?

14 Tom tried to blackmail which *Emmerdale* gossip about her son Peter?

15 Who faked a pregnancy and told Carl that he was the father?

16 How did Max King die?

17 Carl had a relationship with which *Emmerdale* policewoman?

18 Louise Appleton had relationships with which two members of the King family?

19 Who did Carl cheat for information on a contract by joining Tate Haulage as a driver?

20 Who killed Tom King?

Answers on page 211

The Sugdens

1 What was the name of Joe and Jack Sugden's mother: Annie, Amy or Audrey?

2 Where did Andy Sugden first meet Katie: in The Woolpack, in detention at school or at Home Farm?

3 How was Jack Sugden's eldest son Jackie killed: in a car crash, he was accidentally shot or he fell down a mineshaft?

4 What was the occupation of Jack's wife Sarah: librarian, teacher or doctor?

5 True or false: Jack Sugden had an alternative career as a novelist?

6 Who had an affair with Andy's wife Katie?

7 What is the name of the farm where Andy Sugden lives: Butler's Farm, Andrews' Farm or Fox's Farm?

8 Who accidentally shot Jack?

9 True or false: Victoria Sugden had an imaginary friend called Walter Todd?

10 Who was accidentally killed when the Sugden barn caught fire?

Answers on page 211

11 Who started the fire at the barn?

12 Why was Victoria Sugden suspended from school: she hit a tutor with a canoe paddle, she was caught smoking or she cheated in a test?

13 Who is Andy and Daz's biological father?

14 Robert Sugden was driving the car which led to the death of which *Emmerdale* vet?

15 Who is the mother of Andy's daughter Sarah?

16 Frazer Hines played which member of the Sugden family?

17 Jack had an affair with his brother's stepdaughter. What was her name?

18 Jack's wife Diane suffered from what illness: cancer, heart disease or multiple sclerosis?

19 Annie Sugden married which Woolpack landlord in 1995: Amos Brearly, Mr Wilks or Alan Turner?

20 What is the name of the actor who plays Jack Sugden?

Answers on page 211

Hollyoaks
The Early Years

1 In what year did *Hollyoaks* first appear on TV screens: 1995, 1996 or 1997?

2 *Hollyoaks* is set in which Northern city?

3 Ruth Osborne was married to which member of the Benson family?

4 What was the name of Zara Morgan's goth boyfriend?

5 Who was Lord Kildiggin better known as?

6 Which student was devastated to find out that her vicar father had had an affair?

7 Who used to enter other friend's houses by climbing through the window?

8 Who had a relationship with both Adam and Luke Morgan: Mandy Richardson, Jude Cunningham or Geri Hudson?

9 What was the name of Cindy Cunningham's ironing business?

10 Who had an affair with Kurt Benson and also ended up snogging her brother?

11 Ollie Benson died from injuries from what type of accident: car crash, motorbike crash or a helicopter crash?

12 Eco warrior Gina Patrick's first relationship was with which fellow college student: Emily, Anna or Izzy?

13 Dig It! was the name of whose gardening business?

14 Who died after her drink was spiked at Lucy Benson's 18th birthday party?

15 Which wrong 'un spiked the drink?

16 Who was the original owner of Parker's Restaurant?

17 What was the name of Mandy and Lewis Richardson's abusive father: David, Dennis or Derek?

18 Who had a child called Holly?

19 Luke Morgan was bullied and raped by which despicable footballer: Mark, John or Anthony Gibbs?

20 Carol Groves believed that she had which gift: she was psychic, she could heal people or she could see into the future?

Answers on page 211

Hollyoaks
The New Millennium

1 Who bought the Drive 'n' Buy store from Max Cunningham?

2 Chloe Bruce went out with which college caretaker?

3 Which of the following did Debbie Dean not have a relationship with: Dan Hunter, Darren Osborne or Luke Morgan?

4 Who died on the potholing expedition?

5 Lee Hunter studied which course at Hollyoaks Community College?

6 What was Jack Osborne's job before he became landlord of The Dog?

7 Which character was dubbed 'Cruella de Vil' by Zara Morgan?

8 Who returned to *Hollyoaks* after running away to Ibiza for two years: Ellie Hunter, Lisa Hunter or Beth Morgan?

9 Leo Valentine almost died after choking on what: a sweet, a pretzel or a pork scratching?

10 Who blew up the Dog In The Pond?

Answers on page 211

11 Becca Dean had a relationship with which former school pupil?

12 Who inherited a donkey called Small Fortune?

13 Gilbert 'Gilly' Roach supports which football team?

14 Darren Osborne returned to *Hollyoaks* after spending time in which country: America, Australia or Canada?

15 What was Ben Davies' occupation: policeman, fireman or lifeguard?

16 Which racist thug bullied Darlene and Ali Taylor?

17 Cameron Clark suffered from which condition: Obsessive Compulsive Disorder, agoraphobia or fear of dogs?

18 Who died after his rally car exploded?

19 What was David Burke better known as?

20 Who was falsely imprisoned for the attempted murder of Clare: Warren Fox, Max Cunningham or OB?

Answers on page 211

Hollyoaks
The Modern Era

1 Who came out of the closet at his girlfriend's 18th birthday party?

2 Which budding scientist built a rocket which was broken by Steph and Darren?

3 Who appeared in the fictional TV show *Bid Crazy TV* and got into a fight with the presenter?

4 Who pushed Clare Devine from the balcony at The Loft?

5 What was the name of Becca Dean's son?

6 Hannah Ashworth suffered from which disease?

7 Who killed Sean Kennedy?

8 Aleksander Malota was originally from which country?

9 Which pair were babysitting young Grace Hutchinson when she died of SIDS?

10 Who slammed Zoe Carpenter's hand in a taxi door which meant she couldn't go to film school in New York?

Answers on page 212

11 What was the name of Nancy's boyfriend who left *Hollyoaks* for a new life in Goa in India?

12 How did Becca Dean die?

13 Who burgled and then set fire to Evissa?

14 Whose last minute evidence ensured that Warren wasn't jailed for the attack on Clare?

15 Teen mum Amy was in which band: The Baby Diegos, The Baby Maradonas or The Baby Simeones?

16 True or false: Steph Dean inherited a cow in her late Aunt Reenie's will?

17 Who did Clare Devine kidnap to try and get revenge on Justin?

18 Who was Zoe's stalker?

19 Zara Morgan's family left *Hollyoaks* to live in which country: France, Spain or Greece?

20 Which Big Brother winner appeared as an extra on the show?

Answers on page 212

QUIZ 42

Max and OB

1 What was the name of Max's scheming wife?

2 What is OB's full name?

3 What did Tony give Max and OB as a Christmas present?

4 What is the name of Max's young half-brother: Tom, Tony or Tim?

5 Max once opened what type of fast food establishment: burger van, chip shop or curry house?

6 What was the name of OB's on/off girlfriend: Mel Burton, Sophie Burton or Lisa Hunter?

7 Who provided the vocals on Max and OB's CD release *Get Down With That Thing*: Kurt Benson, Gordon Cunningham or Steph Dean?

8 True or false: Max saved OB's life in a drowning incident?

9 Max suffered a heart attack after doing what: running a marathon, taking cocaine or having sex?

10 How did Max's father and stepmother die?

Answers on page 212

11 Who did OB lose his virginity to: Chloe, Steph or Lisa?

12 True or false: Max and OB once pretended to be gay to promote a 'gay dads' campaign?

13 OB suffered from an addiction to what: gambling, alcohol or drugs?

14 Who planted drugs on OB to try and stop him revealing her lies to Max?

15 Why were Max and OB harassed by paparazzi photographers outside a local school?

16 True or false: OB fell for a girl on the internet called Roxy?

17 What is the name of Max and OB's juice bar?

18 Max started a relationship with which employee from the juice bar?

19 What is the name of the actor who plays Max?

20 What is the name of the actor who plays OB?

Answers on page 212

Tony Hutchinson

QUIZ 43

1 What is Tony's main occupation: chef, hairdresser or accountant?

2 Who is Tony's long lost brother: Dick, Dom or Dale?

3 Tony had a relationship with which *Hollyoaks* jailbird?

4 What was the name of Tony's fiancée who cancelled the wedding at the last minute: Julie, Jenny or Jerry?

5 Which of the following jobs hasn't Tony had: nightclub owner, student landlord or taxi driver?

6 What was the name of the video shop which Tony opened?

7 On a trip to Barcelona, Tony declared his love for which curly haired brunette: Carol, Kate or Beth?

8 Who was Tony's first boss at Deva: Jack, Gordon or Andy?

9 Tony had a relationship with which much older woman?

10 What was the name of Tony's restaurant: Grub, Gnosh or Greens?

11 Tony helped rescue which character who had been kidnapped by Rob Hawthorne?

Answers on page 212

12 Tony read the eulogy at the funeral of which friend and rival?

13 Which one of Tony's ex girlfriends claimed that she was pregnant with his child but was really just after his money: Tessie, Terrie or Toni?

14 True or false: Tony appeared in the very first episode of *Hollyoaks*?

15 Which charmer had an unlikely relationship with Tony's mum: Finn, Max or Lewis?

16 Tony was engaged to which two women at the same time?

17 Mandy and Tony got married in which European city: Paris, Berlin or Rome?

18 Tony's house was condemned by environmental health after what exploded: a septic tank, a toilet cistern or a boiler?

19 What was the name of Tony and Mandy's daughter?

20 What is the name of the actor who plays Tony Hutchinson?

Answers on page 212

The McQueens

1 How many McQueen daughters are there in total: four, five or six?

2 What is Nana McQueen's first name: Marigold, Marjorie or Miriam?

3 What are the names of all the McQueen daughters?

4 Which two McQueens got married on the same day?

5 When did John Paul first reveal that he was gay: at his girlfriend's 18th birthday party, at the gym or while on holiday?

6 Tony snogged which McQueen shortly after breaking up with Jacqui?

7 Jacqui was involved in a sham wedding with which Albanian immigrant?

8 John Paul had a relationship with which DJ?

9 Mercedes threatened to sue which beautician after a massage at Evissa?

10 Who dumped Michaela McQueen by text message saying that he only went with her because she was easy?

Answers on page 212

11 John Paul and his partner planned to start a new life in which city: Dublin, Belfast or Edinburgh?

12 John Paul had a relationship with which of the following: Craig Dean, Darren Osborne or Malachy Fisher?

13 Russ Owen sold what item to buy a car for Myra: a wakeboard, a skateboard or a bike?

14 Last minute evidence from Mercedes saved which *Hollyoaks* bad boy from a lifetime in prison?

15 John Paul and Carmel ended up in hospital after breathing in what noxious fumes from a faulty boiler?

16 Mercedes went behind Russ's back and slept with which lover on Tina's hen night?

17 Which McQueen enjoys acting out scenes from her favourite books with her partner?

18 John Paul McQueen is a big football fan but what team does he support: Liverpool, Everton or Chester City?

19 Which of the McQueen sisters once said she'd like to be a nun?

20 Which of the McQueens had an affair with her sister's husband?

Answers on page 212

Home and Away
The First 10 Years

1 In what year did *Home and Away* first appear on UK TV screens: 1988, 1989 or 1990?

2 Who were Tom and Pippa's original foster children?

3 What was the name of Neville's psychic wife who lived on the caravan park: Floss, Candy or Floella?

4 Marilyn Chambers ran which Summer Bay establishment?

5 What was the name of Donald Fisher's surfer son who died on the beach from an aneurysm?

6 Who was Pippa's second husband?

7 Who started the bush fire which caused havoc in Summer Bay: Jack Wilson, Matt Wilson or Tracy Wilson?

8 What is the name of Colleen Smart's only son?

9 Chloe was married to which member of the Fraser family: Lachlan, James or Edward?

10 Which of Pippa's foster children gave birth to a daughter called Tamara?

Answers on page 212

11 Angel ended up in a wheelchair after being hit by which driver: Alf, Ailsa or Fisher?

12 Ailsa suffered a breakdown and saw a ghostly reincarnation of which character?

13 What was Peter O'Neale better known as?

14 Who accidentally blew up a caravan after discarding a cigarette at Shane's bucks night?

15 Selina was abducted by which cult leader while on the way to her wedding?

16 Who murdered Irene's ex-husband, Mud, and threw Steven Matheson from a cliff?

17 What catastrophic event destroyed Alf's Store, Summer Bay High and Angel's house: a flood, a tidal wave or an earthquake?

18 Which psychiatrist was Chloe's attacker?

19 What was the occupation of Fisher's mother Isobel Du Pre: opera singer, actress or musician?

20 Which couple got married on the beach: Travis and Rebecca, Shane and Angel or Will and Gypsy?

Answers on page 212

Home and Away
The New Millennium

1 Which of the Sutherland children suffered from an eating disorder?

2 Who replaced Donald Fisher as Principal after the school lock-in protest: Paris Burnett, London Burnett or Rome Burnett?

3 Which Summer Bay High student took Sally and a group of classmates hostage?

4 Mumma Rose was the head of which cult?

5 What unusual items of clothing die Will and Gypsy wear at their wedding: Hawaiian shirts, cowboy hats or flared trousers?

6 Who was revealed as the Summer Bay stalker?

7 What do Jack Holden, Joel Nash, Ken Harper and Ashton Nader have in common?

8 Who trod on a syringe while doing a nude dare on a camping trip with Kim and Tasha?

9 What was the name of Josh West's controversial construction development: Project 56, Project 57 or Project 58?

10 Who hid Sally's OCD pills, had an affair with Jesse and falsely accused Nick Smith of assaulting her?

11 Who wore a kilt at his wedding?

12 True or false: Henry Hunter left Summer Bay to take up a place at a tap dancing school?

13 Who held a group of Summer Bay residents hostage at Leah's house?

14 Why was Ric expelled from Summer Bay High?

15 Who rescued Hayley from the fire at The Palace?

16 Which character shares a name with the first black player to play football for England?

17 Who was Summer Bay's first goth?

18 Belle, Matilda, Lucas and Ric played what saucy game?

19 Who tried to poison Irene with mercury and attempted to have her put in a mental institution?

20 What is the name of Leah Patterson's son?

Answers on page 213

Home and Away
The Modern Age

QUIZ 47

1 Which innocent youngster was sentenced to 18 years for murdering Rocco Cooper but was later released?

2 How did Emily Armstrong die?

3 Who made her *Home and Away* debut in 2005 arriving on the beach riding a jet ski?

4 Drew Curtis had relationships with which mother and daughter?

5 Which Summer Bay cop failed to mention his wife and two children when he started a relationship with Martha?

6 Teacher Naomi Preston had relationships with which father and son?

7 Who posed as a nude model for an art class?

8 Robbie, Tash and baby Ella left Summer Bay for which country after he was acquitted of murder: England, America or New Zealand?

9 Who is Martha McKenzie's biological mother?

10 Why did Matilda Hunter split from her boyfriend Dean?

11 Which supposed murder victim turned up alive and well to rescue his son from a tense hostage situation?

12 True or false: Hugh Sullivan left Australia to work in Africa?

13 What is the name of the pole dancing club in Summer Bay?

14 Who is the owner of the pole dancing club?

15 Sally was shocked to see that vagrant Miles had written which word on the beach: Milco, Wilco or Bilko?

16 Who unexpectedly inherited $1 million after the death of his grandmother?

17 How did Beth Hunter die?

18 Which Summer Bay resident was married to a murderer called Shane Deeks?

19 What did Kelli Vale do to Amanda which resulted in a terrible car crash: she let down a tyre, she spiked a drink or she cut a brake cable?

20 Leah returned to Greece after her brother had been arrested for what offence: drugs possession, murder or robbery?

Answers on page 213

Home and Away Deaths

1 How did Bobby Simpson die: leukaemia, a car crash or a boating accident?

2 Who caused the death of Angie Russell: Nick, Dylan or Dani?

3 Who was shot dead by constable Terri Garner?

4 How did Tom Fletcher die?

5 Who shot Noah Lawson?

6 The Guv died from heart failure in whose arms: Alf Stewart's, Donald Fisher's or Sally Fletcher's?

7 Which character died after being eaten by a shark: Rory Heywood, Alan Fisher or Philip Matheson?

8 How did Italian exchange student Laura Bonetti die: she ran in front of a train, her car crashed or she drowned?

9 Grigg was found dead in whose car: Alf Stewart's, Donald Fisher's or Sally Fletcher's?

10 Bruce Campbell collapsed and died shortly after watching who play rugby?

Answers on page 213

11 Which member of the Parrish family died of blood poisoning after a motorbike crash: Nick, Shane or Angel?

12 Who died after being struck over the head by the Summer Bay Stalker: Marc Edwards, Joy Foxton or Sarah Lewis?

13 Who was imprisoned for dangerous driving after the death of Chloe Richards?

14 Who drowned while trying to save the life of Sam Marshall: Peter Moss, Michael Ross or Gary Samuels?

15 Which Summer Bay teacher shot Josh West?

16 Who turned off Graham Walters' life support machine?

17 Who died after taking an overdose of crystal meth?

18 How did Alf Stewart's wife Ailsa die: heart attack, she fell from a cliff or a car crash?

19 Flynn Saunders died from what form of cancer: skin, stomach or prostate?

20 Stephanie Mboto died after falling off what: a cliff, a car park roof or a motorbike?

Answers on page 213

Around Summer Bay

QUIZ 49

1 What is the nearest major city to Summer Bay: Sydney, Melbourne or Brisbane?

2 What is the full name of The Diner?

3 What is the name of the house which Irene lives in: The Beach House, The Town House or The Palace?

4 The bar in *Home and Away* is named after which ill-fated character?

5 How many children did the Fletchers originally foster: three, four or five?

6 What is the name of the gym in *Home and Away*?

7 Who did the Fletchers buy the Caravan Park from: Alf Stewart, Don Fisher or Morag Bellingham?

8 Which famous *Home and Away* venue was burnt down by a rebellious teenager?

9 What is the name of the closest town to Summer Bay: Abbey Creek, Yabbie Creek or Gabby Creek?

10 Who were the original owners of The Diner?

Answers on page 213

11 What is the name of the church in Summer Bay: St James', St Peter's or St Alf's?

12 What is the name of the real town used for filming most of the exteriors for the series?

13 Where in Sydney did Irene and Dylan find Angie's cousin Josie: a brothel, a convent or a casino?

14 Alf Stewart opened a fishing bait store with which character?

15 Who burnt down the boatshed in revenge for an accident Dylan suffered while working there?

16 Where did Kim have his bucks party?

17 What entertainment was provided at Kim's bucks party: karaoke, a stripper or a poker night?

18 Who was the original principal of Summer Bay High?

19 Which character stole Beth's keys to the Surf Club: Lucas, Robbie or Ric?

20 Which of the following has not lived in the Stewart House: Aaron Welles, Mitch McColl or Vinnie Patterson?

Answers on page 213

Donald Fisher

1 What is Donald Fisher's profession: teacher, doctor or businessman?

2 Fisher was married to the sister of which long term Summer Bay resident?

3 What was the name of Fisher's long lost mother who returned to Summer Bay in 1997: Isobel, Nellie or Ivana?

4 Fisher helped which young tearaway become a successful artist?

5 What is Fisher's nickname?

6 Fisher's son Adam died from an aneurysm after an accident doing what activity: surfing, sailing or playing cricket?

7 Who did Fisher's daughter Rebecca marry?

8 What was the name of Fisher's tomboy daughter?

9 Who was the mother of this surprise daughter?

10 Why was Fisher once arrested: dangerous driving, being involved in a sit-in at the school or fraud?

Answers on page 213

11 After a DNA test who was confirmed as Fisher's grandson: Seb, Duncan or David?

12 What was the name of Fisher's second wife?

13 Fisher had a relationship with which kleptomaniac?

14 True or false: Donald Fisher is also the name of the founder of clothes store Gap?

15 How did Fisher's son Byron die: car crash, cancer or plane crash?

16 Fisher became close friends with which policeman who was the boyfriend of his niece Lucinda?

17 What did Fisher have the honour of carrying in the run-up to the 2000 Olympic Games?

18 Fisher left Summer Bay to take up what kind of business: hotel, vineyard or farm?

19 What was the name of the book that Fisher wrote?

20 What is the name of the actor who plays Donald Fisher?

Answers on page 213

Sally Fletcher

1 What was the name of Sally Fletcher's husband?

2 What is Sally's daughter called?

3 Sally was engaged to which Irishman who had an affair with Gypsy?

4 Which of the following hasn't Sally had a relationship with: Vinnie, Brad or Dan?

5 What was Sally's imaginary friend called?

6 True or false: Sally once suffered from Obsessive Compulsive Disorder?

7 How did Sally's biological parents die: boating accident, plane crash or car crash?

8 What is the name of Sally's adoptive daughter?

9 Which schoolboy tried to frame Sally by claiming that he was having an affair with her?

10 What is the name of Sally's adoptive son?

Answers on page 214

11 Who caught Sally at a drunken beach party: Alf, Pippa or Fisher?

12 What was the name of the surrogate mother who gave birth to Sally's child?

13 What subject does Sally teach: history, geography or biology?

14 Sally was the manageress of which burger bar?

15 At university, Sally studied what subject?

16 Sally suffered from which form of cancer: breast cancer, ovarian cancer or skin cancer?

17 Who was the teacher Sally had a relationship with after Flynn died?

18 What was the name of the stalker who kidnapped Sally?

19 Sally was attacked by gang member Rocco in 2006. What did he do to her: stab her, shoot her or run her over?

20 What is the name of the actress who plays Sally?

Answers on page 214

Alf Stewart

1 Alf has been married twice. What were the names of his two wives?

2 What was the name of the bait shop owned by Alf?

3 Alf did a spell in prison for what offence: fraud, drunken disorderly or dangerous driving?

4 What is the name of Alf's son: Damian, Duncan or Daniel?

5 One of Alf's sisters was married to which Summer Bay stalwart: Donald Fisher, Tom Fletcher or Tony Holden?

6 What is the name of Alf's boat?

7 Who did Alf run over while driving his Ute?

8 Alf has one granddaughter. What is her name?

9 True or false: Alf owned a liquor store?

10 What is Alf's middle name: Douglas, Donald or David?

Answers on page 214

11 How did Alf's second wife die: cancer, heart attack or car crash?

12 What is the name of Alf's daughter: Roo, Rebecca or Rachel?

13 True of false: Alf once owned Bonza Burgers?

14 When Alf was depressed he made decisions using what object: a coin, a deck of cards or a lucky rabbit's foot?

15 Alf is in charge of which voluntary organisation?

16 True or false: Alf appeared in the first ever episode of *Home and Away*?

17 What is the name of Alf's grandson?

18 How many sisters does Alf have?

19 What are the names of his sisters?

20 What is the name of the actor who plays Alf?

Answers on page 214

Neighbours The 1980s

1 In what year was *Neighbours* first shown in the UK?

2 What was the occupation of Jim Robinson's wife Beverley?

3 What was the name of Max Ramsay's wife: Anna, Maria or Martha?

4 Hollywood star Guy Pearce played which Ramsay Street regular?

5 Who made her *Neighbours* debut trying to break into the Ramsay house: Charlene, Jane or Nikki?

6 The opening credits featured the Ramsay Street regulars playing which game: football, darts or cricket?

7 Who wrote an agony aunt column in the local newspaper called 'Dear Georgette'?

8 As well as being a doctor, Clive Gibbons ran what unlikely business?

9 Which character was best known for her squealing laugh and for her collection of porcelain pigs?

10 What was Des Clarke's occupation?

11 Which Ramsay Street resident was an accomplished high board diver?

12 Who killed her father Charles and also shot husband Paul Robinson?

13 Jane Harris was the granddaughter of which Ramsay Street gossip?

14 What was the name of Des and Daphne's son: Jamie, Toby or Todd?

15 Which Ramsay Street resident took up fortune-telling?

16 Clive Gibbons had to perform an emergency operation on which youngster who had been stung by a wasp?

17 Craig McLachlan played which Erinsborough DJ?

18 Which pair of sisters moved in with Mrs Mangel in 1988?

19 Who started a chauffeur service called Home James?

20 What was the name of Todd Landers' younger sister: Katie, Kirsten or Kerry?

Answers on page 214

Neighbours The 1990s

1 Which husband and wife went on a European tour after winning the lottery?

2 What was Wayne Reeves better known as?

3 Paul Robinson married which Alessi twin?

4 What was the name of Lou Carpenter's womanising eldest son: Guy, Glen or Gary?

5 What religious name did Mark Gottlieb give The Coffee Shop?

6 Amy Greenwood tried to convince Lance Wilkinson that what activity would be good for their relationship: aerobics, a pampering weekend or ballroom dancing?

7 Who was arrested on suspicion of murdering a patient: Karl Kennedy, Pam Willis or Beverley Marshall?

8 Philip Martin married which physiotherapist?

9 Which pair of rivals had to be rescued from the bush after a plane crash?

10 Who was the cheeky cockney chappy who briefly lived with the Bishops: Eddie Buckingham, Eddie Balmoral or Eddie Sandringham?

Answers on page 214

11 Which pair of luckless lovers appeared on a TV show called *Dream Date*?

12 What was the name of Phoebe's daughter: Faith, Hope or Charity?

13 Who was arrested at his wife Julie's funeral?

14 Brett Stark accompanied Susan Kennedy on a trip to which African country: Kenya, Morocco or Zimbabwe?

15 Dorothy Burke worked at which Erinsborough establishment?

16 Libby Kennedy dated which University lecturer?

17 True or false: Lucy Robinson worked as a go-go dancer?

18 Who cancelled her wedding to Brad Willis after finding him in bed with Lauren Carpenter?

19 Which family's house caught fire on Millennium Eve with Lolly Carpenter still inside?

20 Who admitted that she had helped her sick mother to die?

Answers on page 214

Neighbours Present Day

1 The Parker family took in an orphaned Kangaroo. What did they call him?

2 Who unexpectedly died at Janelle's birthday party?

3 Why was young Kerry Mangel's birth especially difficult: there was a fire at the hospital, she was born in a barn or the hospital had run out of drugs?

4 Newlyweds Janelle and Allan Steiger left Erinsborough by what means of transport: hot air balloon, pony and trap or helicopter?

5 Who went on the run after knocking over and killing Cameron Robinson?

6 What was the name of Ned Parker's ex-girlfriend who turned up on his doorstep to tell him he had an eight-year-old son?

7 Who took Katya, Steph, Zeke and baby Charlie hostage?

8 Who was shot trying to rescue the hostages?

9 Katya left Ramsay Street to work as a medic for what type of organisation: a charity, a cricket team or an Aussie Rules football team?

10 Who did Elle Robinson find Dylan Timmins in bed with on a Valentine's Day retreat?

11 Karl and Susan bumped into which Spice Girl on their trip to London?

12 Who stalked and later kidnapped Pepper Steiger?

13 The ill-fated plane flight over Tasmania had what special theme: 1940s, 1960s or 1980s?

14 What was the name of the crooked spiritualist who claimed he could channel the spirit of Stingray?

15 Which pair shared Ramsay Street's first lesbian kiss?

16 True or false: there's a nightclub in Erinsborough called Hemisfear?

17 How was Frazer Yeats paralysed: in a car crash, he fell from a cliff or he was trampled by a horse?

18 The Brown brothers were named after members of which band?

19 Why did Harold's love interest Loris Timmins leave Ramsay Street: to find her granddaughter, to escape the police or to work for charity overseas?

20 Max was injured in the Lassiter's fire searching for what: a missing person, Madge's cookbook or some money?

Answers on page 214

Neighbours Deaths

1 How did Jim Robinson die: heart attack, cancer or a car crash?

2 Who briefly came out of a coma to say 'I love you too, Clarkey' before dying of a cardiac arrest?

3 How did Drew Kirk die?

4 Madge Bishop's final request was for Paul and Harold to take a trip to which city: London, Paris or Rome?

5 Who died just weeks after he'd tied the knot with Helen Daniels?

6 Cheryl Stark died after being given morphine by which doctor?

7 How did Gus Cleary die: he was murdered, a car crash he drowned?

8 Who died after getting shot while protesting against a duck shoot?

9 How did David, Liljana and Serena Bishop die?

10 Who was thought to have drowned but made a surprise re-appearance some years later?

11 Who died in a drag race with Rick Alessi?

12 How did Dee Bliss die: car crash, plane crash or accidental overdose?

13 Who died just moments after watching a video of Scott and Charlene's wedding which settled a feud between the Robinsons and Ramsays?

14 Which elderly campaigner left her house to Anne Wilkinson after she died: Lily, Betty or Edna Madigan?

15 Who was knocked over and killed crossing a busy road while trying to stop his young girlfriend from having an abortion?

16 Which member of the Willis family died after being shot by criminals: Cody, Adam or Brad?

17 What was the name of Tess Bell's abusive husband who died after crashing his car into Steph Scully's motorbike: Brendan, Brandon or Bradford?

18 Who died at a Murder Mystery Weekend: Julie Martin, Helen Daniels or Pam Willis?

19 Who went to live with his father Joe Mangel after the death of his mother Noelene?

20 Which economics professor died from leukaemia?

Answers on page 215

Around Erinsborough

QUIZ 57

1 *Neighbours* is set in which Australian city: Melbourne, Sydney or Brisbane?

2 The show is based on the residents of which street?

3 Which member of the Robinson family was the original owner of Lassiters?

4 What is the name of the venue which was formerly known as the Scarlet Bar: Chelsea's, Charlie's or Chester's?

5 What was the original name or Erinsborough's favourite pub: The Waterhole, Chez Chez or Lou's Place?

6 What is the name of Erinsborough's fast food restaurant: Grease Monkeys, Erinsborough Diner or Fat Jack's?

7 Madge Bishop played for the Grey Growlers. What sport did they play: bowls, cricket or basketball?

8 The General Store used to be what famous Erinsborough landmark?

9 Conor O'Neil worked in which swim and surf shop: Bounce, Splash or Waves?

10 What is the name of the prison that has housed Lou Carpenter, Darcy Tyler and Dylan Timmins?

Answers on page 215

11 Toadfish was a successful DJ on which radio station?

12 Who was the manager of the bar Chez Chez: Lou Carpenter, Paul Robinson or Cheryl Stark?

13 The pupils at Erinsborough High School wear what colour uniforms: purple, yellow or green?

14 Drew Kirk, Steph Scully and Stuart Parker all worked at which garage?

15 What was the name of the hair salon owned by Gino Esposito?

16 Number 30 Ramsay Street was given what name by Toadie, Stuart and Conor?

17 Where did the Timmins family stay after being evicted from the Scully household?

18 What is the name of Erinsborough's local newspaper?

19 Which of the following isn't a nearby suburb to Erinsborough: Anson's Corner, Eden Hills or Heartridge?

20 What number was the house that the Robinsons and later the Scullys and Parkers lived at: 13, 26 or 39?

Answers on page 215

Harold and Lou

1 Harold tried to kill which Ramsay Street bad boy?

2 What is the name of Lou's adoptive daughter?

3 How many times has Lou been married?

4 What are the names of all of Lou's wives?

5 What is the name of Harold's granddaughter: Sun, Sea or Sky?

6 What nickname did Lou give to Harold: Telly Tubby, Jelly Belly or Roly Poly?

7 Harold didn't have a relationship with which of the following: Ruby Dwyer, Svetlanka Ristic or Mrs Mangel?

8 What are the names of Lou's three biological children?

9 True or false: Lou donated a kidney to Harold?

10 Where was Harold in the years when he had lost his memory: England, Tasmania or New Zealand?

11 What are the names of Harold's two children?

12 What was the name of Lou's Russian internet lover: Mishka, Valentina or Petra?

13 Lou became a champion at what unlikely activity: Dungeons and Dragons, online poker or ballroom dancing?

14 After disappearing, Harold started working for the Salvation Army using what name: Ted, Tom or Tony?

15 Lou was engaged to which blonde bombshell?

16 Which pair dreamed up the Afro Harold advertising campaign: Lori and Connor or Toady and Sheena?

17 Lou and Harold battled for the romantic attentions of which clergywoman?

18 Harold was a foster father to which two boys?

19 What is the name of the actor who plays Harold?

20 What is the name of the actor who plays Lou?

Answers on page 215

The Kennedys

1 What is Karl Kennedy's profession: doctor, dentist or lawyer?

2 What is the name of Karl's elderly father: Tom, Dick or Harry?

3 What is Susan Kennedy's profession: teacher, lawyer or doctor?

4 How many children do Karl and Susan have together: two, three or four?

5 What was the name of Libby's late husband?

6 Malcolm Kennedy shot which neighbour in the leg shortly after arriving in Ramsay Street?

7 What was the name of the secretary who Karl had his first affair with: Sarah Beaumont, Jane Harris or Ruth Martin?

8 What was the name of Susan's nephew who worked alongside Karl?

9 What was Billy Kennedy's occupation: carpenter, plumber or electrician?

10 Susan had a relationship with which man of the cloth?

Answers on page 215

11 How did Susan develop amnesia: she banged her head after slipping on some milk, she was in a car crash or she suffered from a stroke?

12 What is the name of Libby's son?

13 Susan married which patient of Karl's but was widowed shortly after?

14 Karl fathered a daughter with which Ramsay Street schemer?

15 What was Susan's maiden name: Smith, Jones or Jackson?

16 Karl and Susan remarried in 2007. The priest who married them was played by which English actor: Neil Morrissey, Harry Enfield or Martin Clunes?

17 What was the name of the coffee shop company which Mal worked for: Cuppa Diem, Hot Coffee or Teas Please?

18 True or false: Karl sang in a kids' band called Oodles O'Noodles?

19 Karl proposed to Susan at which London tourist attraction: the London Eye, the Tower of London or St Paul's Cathedral?

20 Which singing star was a surprise witness at Karl and Susan's remarriage: Kim Wilde, Sinitta or Sonia?

Answers on page 215

The Robinsons

QUIZ 60

1 What was the name of Jim Robinson's mother-in-law who moved in and helped run the family home?

2 Scott Robinson married which next door neighbour?

3 Jim was married to which Erinsborough doctor?

4 What are the names of Paul Robinson's five children?

5 Who is the mother of Paul Robinson's triplets: Gail, Terry or Christina?

6 Which member of the Robinson family was an airline steward?

7 Terry Inglis was married to which member of the Robinson clan?

8 Julie Robinson was married to which Ramsay Street bank manager?

9 What was the name of Jim's youngest child?

10 Who planted the bomb which exploded on the Bass Strait flight?

11 Who accidentally ran over and killed Cameron Robinson?

Answers on page 215

12 Elle Robinson took a shine to which innocent illiterate?

13 What was the name of Jim's long lost son: Glen, Gary or Gordon?

14 Why did Paul have to have his leg amputated: he was thrown from a cliff, he was involved in a car crash or he fell from a horse?

15 Paul Robinson often had dealings with which Japanese businessman: Mr Udugawa, Mr Matsui or Mr Ichiro?

16 What was the name of the young artist who moved into the Robinson household: Nick Page, Brett Stark or Ryan McLachlan?

17 While suffering from a brain tumour, Paul imagined seeing a homeless teenager. What was his name: Fox, Rabbit or Rover?

18 Which gold digger tried to withdraw all of Jim's money while he lay dying on his kitchen floor: Fiona Hartman, Caroline Alessi or Pam Willis?

19 Stefan Dennis plays which member of the Robinson clan?

20 What is the name of the actor who played Jim?

Answers on page 215

Brookside Part One

1 *Brookside* was set in which English city: Leeds, Liverpool or Manchester?

2 What was the character Thomas Sweeney more usually known as?

3 Where was Trevor Jordache buried after he was killed?

4 What was the name of Bobby Grant's wife: Sheila, Susan or Sarah?

5 Barry Grant and Terry Sullivan sometimes did work for which local gangster: Tommy McArdle, Terry McDermott or Tony McNamara?

6 What was the name of Ron Dixon's mobile shop?

7 Who was the cult leader who eventually firebombed number five: Simon Howe, Steven Howe or Shaun Howe?

8 Which pair of characters shared soap's first lesbian kiss?

9 What was the name of the nightclub in *Brookside*: La Luz, La Paz or Las Amigos?

10 Which Close resident had an incestuous relationship with her brother Nat?

Answers on page 216

11 Who blew all of her lottery winnings after becoming addicted to gambling?

12 Who shot Clint Moffat: Ron Dixon, Barry Grant or Jimmy Corkhill?

13 Jason and Greg Shadwick were killed after what incident at the Millennium Club: a fire, a shooting or a bomb exploded?

14 Who did Terry Sullivan sell the Pizza Parade to: Mick Johnson, Jimmy Corkhill or Barry Grant?

15 What was the name of the actress who played Beth Jordache?

16 How did Susannah Farnham die: in a fire, in a car crash or by falling down the stairs?

17 Anthony Murray was bullied by which fearsome schoolgirl?

18 Which member of the Nolan Sisters starred in *Brookside*?

19 The first openly gay soap character appeared in *Brookside*. What was his name?

20 What was the name of the actress who played Emily Shadwick?

Answers on page 216

Brookside Part Two

QUIZ 62

1 What were the names of Ron and Debbie Dixon's three children?

2 Which of the following chat show hosts didn't make a guest appearance in Brookside: Michael Parkinson, Russell Harty or Graham Norton?

3 What were the names of Max Farnham's three wives?

4 What was the name of Barry Grant's half-brother?

5 Bryan Murray who played Trevor Jordache played which member of the Boswell family in the BBC comedy *Bread*: Joey, Freddie or Shifty?

6 Margaret Clemens had a relationship with Derrick O'Farrell. What was his unlikely occupation: priest, oil rigger or circus performer?

7 Mick Johnson first moved to Brookside Close as a lodger with which grumpy resident?

8 What was the name of Rachel Jordache's horrible husband: Christian, Charlie or Christopher?

9 Who did Max and Susannah Farnham pay to become a surrogate mother?

10 How did Emily Shadwick die: she was shot, she fell from a window or she was in a car crash?

11 Who killed the frightening school bully Imelda Clough?

12 The actress who played Josie Johnson is the sister of which Olympic gold medalist?

13 Which member of the Shadwick family was a victim of a date rape attack: Nikki, Emily or Margi?

14 Which character left *Brookside* to play football for Torquay United: Tim O'Leary, Geoff Rogers or Jason Shadwick?

15 True or false: David Frost made a guest appearance on the show?

16 Who was the father of Bev McLoughlin's son Josh: Ron Dixon, Mike Dixon or Tony Dixon?

17 Who was the *Brookside* gangster who ran a very shady protection racket: Callum Finnegan, Colman Rushe or Dara Finneran?

18 What was the name of Heather Haversham's drug addict husband who died of an overdose?

19 What was Eddie Banks's most prized possession: a Harley-Davidson motorbike, a Rolls Royce or a speedboat?

20 Phil Redmond, the creator of *Brookside* was also the man behind which long-running children's drama?

Answers on page 216

The Corkhills

1 How were Billy and Jimmy Corkhill related: brothers, cousins or uncle and nephew?

2 Jimmy Corkhill was addicted to what: alcohol, gambling or drugs?

3 What was the name of Jimmy Corkhill's wife: Jackie, Jenny or Julie?

4 Which Corkhill was sacked from his job for punching a teacher after he found out his daughter was having an affair?

5 Jimmy Corkhill was the father of three children. What were their names?

6 What was Rod Corkhill's occupation?

7 Lyndsey Corkhill had a relationship with which hairdresser?

8 What was the name of Jimmy Corkhill's shop on Brookside Parade: Cheap and Cheerful, Kowboy Kutz, or Crash Bang Wallop?

9 Who was married to Bobby Grant and then Billy Corkhill?

10 Jimmy Corkhill set up a taxi firm. What was it called?

Answers on page 216

11 What was Tracy Corkhill's occupation?

12 Who did Jackie Corkhill have an affair with: Ron Dixon, Mike Dixon or DD Dixon?

13 What was the name of Jimmy Corkhill's Staffordshire Bull Terrier: Cracker, Ringo or Koppite?

14 Jimmy Corkhill was involved in a car crash which led to the death of which neighbour?

15 What was the name of Lindsey Corkhill's daughter: Kylie, Dannii or Britney?

16 Who did Rod Corkhill marry: Diana, Debbie or Denise Spence?

17 What was the name of Lindsey Corkhill's lesbian lover?

18 Actress Clare Sweeney played which member of the Corkhill clan?

19 True or false: one of Jimmy Corkhill's many jobs was as a maths teacher?

20 The role of Jimmy Corkhill was played by which actor?

Answers on page 216

Crossroads

QUIZ 64

1 *Crossroads* was set on the outskirts of which city: Birmingham, Leeds or Nottingham?

2 Benny was famous for wearing what item of clothing: a woolly hat, a baseball cap or a trilby?

3 In what decade did *Crossroads* first appear on TV screens: 1960s, 1970s or 1980s?

4 Which flame-haired matriarch was the original owner of *Crossroads*?

5 What were the first names of the Hunters, the husband and wife team which ran *Crossroads*?

6 Who was the object of Benny's affections: Miss Debbie, Miss Doreen or Miss Diane?

7 Which *Coronation Street* actress also appeared in *Crossroads* as waitress Marilyn Gates: Sue Nicholls, Anne Kirkbride or Lynne Perrie?

8 How was the Motel almost destroyed in 1981: a fire, a tanker explosion or a terrible storm?

9 Long-serving cleaner Doris Luke was played by which actress, most famous for playing Nora Batty in *Last Of The Summer Wine*?

10 Who tried to poison Meg for the insurance money: Malcolm Ryder or Hugh Mortimer?

11 True or false: the Scottish chef at *Crossroads* was called Shughie McFee?

12 Meg left *Crossroads* for a new life on what glamorous mode of transport: Concorde, The QE2 or a Rolls Royce?

13 What was the name of Jill Chance's moustachioed husband: Adam, Alex or Alan?

14 True or false: David Jason, better known as Del Boy, appeared in *Crossroads* as Bert Bradshaw?

15 Which ex-girlfriend of Beatle Paul McCartney, played the bitchy hotel owner Angel Samson?

16 Which character spoke the opening and closing lines in the first and last episodes of the original series?

17 Which of the following didn't make a guest appearance on the show: Bob Monkhouse, Ken Dodd or Ronnie Barker?

18 *Crossroads* was set in which fictional suburb: King's Oak, Queen's Oak or Prince's Oak?

19 Which band covered the theme music to *Crossroads*: Wings, ELO or Slade?

20 Which former Prime Minister was said to be a massive fan of the show: Harold Wilson, Ted Heath or Margaret Thatcher?

Answers on page 216

Dallas

1 *Dallas* was set in which American state: Texas, California or Florida?

2 The show centred on the trials and tribulations of which two families?

3 J.R. was played by which actor?

4 What was the name of the Ewing ranch?

5 Patrick Duffy played which character in *Dallas*?

6 What was the name of J.R.'s arch nemesis: John Barnes, Peter Barnes or Cliff Barnes?

7 How many children did Jock Ewing have: two, three or four?

8 What was J.R.'s wife called: Sue Ellen, Pamela or Valerie?

9 True or false: Brad Pitt appeared in *Dallas*?

10 Legendary actress Barbara Bel Geddes played which character in *Dallas*?

Answers on page 216

11 Which of Sue Ellen's lovers did J.R. push off a balcony?

12 What was Miss Ellie's second husband called: Clayton Farlow, Chris Farlow or Clayton Blackmore?

13 What was Gary and Val's daughter called?

14 What was the nickname of Willard Barnes: Digger, Bigger or Rigger?

15 What do the letters J.R. in J.R. Ewing stand for?

16 Pam Ewing was severely injured after being involved in what: a road accident, a plane crash or a motorbike fall?

17 Which character was dubbed 'The Poison Dwarf' by Terry Wogan?

18 Who was resurrected in a shower after being killed off in the previous series?

19 Which Dynasty star was originally offered the part of Pam?

20 Who shot J.R.?

Answers on page 216

Dynasty

1 *Dynasty* was set in which American city: Denver, Detroit or Dallas?

2 Which star of *Bad Girls*, *Tenko* and *Strictly Come Dancing* appeared in *Dynasty*?

3 What was the name of the main family in *Dynasty*?

4 Linda Evans played which character: Krystle, Diamond or Ruby?

5 True or false: George Peppard was originally chosen to play Blake Carrington?

6 What was the name of the character played by Joan Collins?

7 The role of Sammy Jo was played by which blonde bombshell?

8 What was the name of Blake Carrington's gay son?

9 True or false: US President Ronald Reagan appeared in *Dynasty*?

10 Who tried to murder Jeff Colby by painting his office with toxic paint?

11 Blake and Alexis's daughter Amanda married a prince from where: Moldavia, Monrovia or Milton Keynes?

Answers on page 217

12 Kate O'Mara played a character called: Caress, Embrace or Adore?

13 What was the name of Blake and Alexis's scheming daughter?

14 True or false: John Forsythe who played Blake Carrington was also the voice of Charlie in *Charlie's Angels*?

15 Which actor, who is best known for playing Robin Hood, also appeared in *Dynasty*: Michael Praed, Jason Connery or Kevin Costner?

16 The Carringtons made their money in which industry: hotels, oil or shipping?

17 Who did Blake try and strangle at the Carrington Mansion: Alexis, Krystle or Dominique?

18 Alexis and Krystle had the first of their infamous cat fights at which location: Alexis's art studio, the Carrington mansion or a hotel?

19 What was the name of the horse that Blake gave to Krystle: Allegre, Alhambra or Amazon?

20 Which character was kidnapped as a baby and grew up with the name Michael Torrance?

Answers on page 217

QUIZ 67 Eldorado

1 *Eldorado* was set in which country?

2 What was the name of the part-time club singer: Trish Valentine, Trish Scorpio or Trish Gemini?

3 Actor Jesse Birdsall played which *Eldorado* bad boy?

4 How long was *Eldorado* on air for: one month, six months or one year?

5 What was the name of the resort in *Eldorado*: Los Amigos, Los Barcos or Los Carbos?

6 *Eldorado* filled the time slot vacated by which chat show: Wogan, Parkinson or Harty?

7 What was the name of the restaurant in *Eldorado*: Georgio's, Gianluca's or Giovanni's?

8 Which character served a prison sentence for GBH: Drew, Marcus or Sandy?

9 How many episodes of *Eldorado* were produced: 12, 156 or 166?

10 *Eldorado* actor Derek Martin went on to play which taxi driver in *EastEnders*?

11 True or false: there was a character in *Eldorado* called Bunny?

Answers on page 217

12 The theme tune to *Eldorado* was called *When You Call*, *When You Go Away* or *When You Love Me*?

13 What was the name of Marcus's Spanish girlfriend: Pilar, Irene or Simona?

14 Campbell Morrison, who played Drew Lockhead in *Eldorado*, also appeared as what in *EastEnders*: a vicar, a policeman or a doctor?

15 True or false: *Eldorado* came 11th in Channel 4 programme *The 100 TV Moments From Hell*?

16 What was the name of the character played by Kathy Pitkin: Poppy, Fizz or Splash?

17 Which of the following wasn't a family in the show: the Webb family, the Fernandez family or the Butler family?

18 What was the name of the bar in the resort: Jan's, Joy's or Jay's Bar?

19 What were the names of the two Lockhead children: Nessa and Brown, Nessa and Blair or Nessa and Cameron?

20 Jesse Birdsall is married to the actress who played which *Only Fools and Horses* character: Marlene, Cassandra or Raquel?

Answers on page 217

Family Affairs

QUIZ 68

1 *Family Affairs* was broadcast on which TV channel?

2 Who died in a car crash just minutes after marrying Angus Hart?

3 What was the name of the pub which Pete Callan bought in 2000: The White Swan, The Black Swan or The Grey Swan?

4 In 2000 the focus of *Family Affairs* moved to which street: Sidney Street, Stanley Street or Sofia Street?

5 What was the name of the biggest bad boy in *Family Affairs*: Pete Callan, Geoff Callow or Barry Vaughan?

6 Which member of the Trip family was involved in an armed robbery on a Post Office?

7 *Family Affairs* was originally set in which fictional Kent town: Charnham, Chelnam or Charlsford?

8 Which brassy barmaid slept with Duncan Hart and then later with his sister Holly?

9 Who was Dave Matthews's chain smoking wife: Cat, Kay or Chris?

10 Which character was noted for her outrageous facial piercings?

Answers on page 217

11 Who was the owner of the mini supermarket: Dusty McHugh, Curly McHugh or Dinky McHugh?

12 Which family owned the sandwich shop: The Davenports, The Costellos or The Harts?

13 What was the name of the bar in *Family Affairs*: The Cock, The Lock or The Stock?

14 Who died in a fire at the corner cafe in 2003?

15 Which famous nightclub owner made a guest appearance in *Family Affairs*?

16 Who murdered Josh Matthews and then framed his then wife Siobhan?

17 Who was the French sounding alter ego of chef Dudley Starr: Serge Pompidou, Francois Chirac or Jean-Claude Fradin?

18 What was Max Derwin's occupation?

19 Gary Webster, who played Gary Costello, had previously appeared in which successful drama: *Minder*, *The Sweeney* or *The Professionals*?

20 Stephen Yardley, better known as Ken Masters from *Howards' Way*, played which character in *Family Affairs*?

Answers on page 217

Prisoner Cell Block H

1 *Prisoner* was set in which Australian prison?

2 Who replaced Erica Davidson as Prison Governor: Ann Reynolds, Ann Haddy or Ann Charleston?

3 Which prison officer was known as Po Face?

4 Which prisoner was known as The Ice Lady: Judy Bryant, Myra Desmond or Sonia Stevens?

5 What was the name of the lesbian prison officer: Joan Ferguson, Jean Ferguson or June Ferguson?

6 Which alcoholic inmate illicitly brewed the lethal drink grog?

7 The most powerful inmate at the prison was given what title: Top Dog, Top Bitch or Queen of the Jungle?

8 Which evil prisoner killed Paddy Lawson while in prison but was later killed herself by Bea Smith?

9 What was the name of the prison's deputy governor: Jim Fletcher, Darren Fletcher or Shane Fletcher?

10 Who died in a fire while trying to recover Joan Ferguson's personal diaries?

11 Which ginger-haired murderer was known as Queen Bea?

12 What was Joan Ferguson's nickname: The Beast, The Freak or The Moan?

13 Ray Proctor had what job at the prison: gardener, chef or doctor?

14 Which character was known as 'vinegar tits'?

15 Doreen Burns was often seen clutching what object: a teddy bear, a blanket or a baby doll?

16 Meg Morris and Ann Reynolds were kidnapped by the crazy relative of which inmate?

17 Which prison warder was the only character to appear in both the first and last episodes of the show?

18 Jenny Hartley continually proclaimed that she was innocent of killing which relative: nana, mother or auntie?

19 True or false: Ian Smith who plays Harold Bishop in *Neighbours* appeared in *Prisoner*?

20 What was the theme tune to *Prisoner* called?

Answers on page 217

Actors

Can you match the actor with the character they played?

1. Nigel Pivaro
2. Leslie Grantham
3. Alan Dale
4. Steve McFadden
5. Wendy Richard
6. Ada Nicodemou
7. Charles Lawson
8. Jessie Wallace
9. James Hooton
10. Jackie Woodburne

11. Eileen Derbyshire
12. Patrick Mower
13. Bill Tarmey
14. Lynne McGranger
15. Dean Sullivan
16. Samantha Janus
17. Ryan Moloney
18. Bryan Mosley
19. Rudolph Walker
20. Chris Chittell

a Irene Roberts

b Susan Kennedy

c Jim McDonald

d Rodney Blackstock

e Emily Bishop

f Patrick Trueman

g Terry Duckworth

h Toadfish Rebecchi

i Jim Robinson

j Alf Roberts

k Pauline Fowler

l Eric Pollard

m Den Watts

n Jack Duckworth

o Kat Slater

p Sam Dingle

q Leah Patterson-Baker

r Phil Mitchell

s Ronnie Mitchell

t Jimmy Corkhill

Answers on page 217

Affairs Part One

1 *Coronation Street's* Ken Barlow and Mike Baldwin were involved in an infamous tug of love for which woman?

2 Which *Neighbour* has had affairs with Karl Kennedy, Paul Robinson, Ned Parker and Pete Gartside?

3 Which *EastEnder* had affairs with Wicksy, hunky lifeguard Matt and David Wicks?

4 Which *Coronation Street* stalwart had an affair with Wendy Crozier: Mike Baldwin, Ken Barlow or Don Brennan?

5 Steve McDonald cheated on wife Karen with which *Coronation Street* temptress?

6 Which *Hollyoaks* character had an affair with Helen, who was married to Mr Cunningham at the time?

7 Janice Battersby broke up with husband Les after an affair with which *Coronation Street* biker?

8 In *EastEnders*, Bianca had an affair with which older man who was also dating her mother?

9 In *Home and Away*, who cheated on Ric with Macca and was later involved with Jules and Henk?

10 Maxine Peacock had an affair with which *Coronation Street* doctor?

Answers on page 218

11 In *Hollyoaks*, which of Tony's friends upset him by having a relationship with his mother: Finn, Max or Ben?

12 Which *EastEnder* had an unlikely affair with Mrs Hewitt?

13 Both Mike Baldwin and his son Mark had affairs with which two-timing gold digger?

14 Which *Emmerdale* schoolgirl had an affair with her teacher, Tom Bainbridge: Kelly Windsor, Emma Cairns or Donna Windsor?

15 *EastEnder* Kathy Beale had an affair with a man in which unlikely occupation: vicar, poet or clown?

16 Who in *Coronation Street* had an affair with mechanic Chris Collins?

17 *Emmerdale's* Bernice cheated on husband Ashley with which Woolpack chef: Carlos, José or Ramon?

18 In *Hollyoaks*, Kurt Benson had an affair with which member of the Patrick family: Sol, Gina or Kate?

19 Which *EastEnder* cheated on his wife Tanya with his son's partner Stacey?

20 Martin Platt's marriage to Gail broke down after he admitted to an affair with which nurse?

Answers on page 218

Affairs Part Two

QUIZ 72

1 How was Stacey and Max Branning's affair revealed: by a text message, by a videotape or via an overheard phone call?

2 Natalie Horrocks had an affair with which Weatherfield mechanic?

3 In *EastEnders* Bianca's marriage to Ricky ended after she found out he'd had an affair with which close friend?

4 Which Erinsborough love rat had relationships with Lucy Robinson, Caroline Alessi and Gaby Willis all at the same time?

5 Lisa Raymond had a naughty affair with which Walford market inspector?

6 Bill Webster cheated on his wife Maureen with which *Coronation Street* veteran?

7 Stacey Slater revealed whose affair: Pat and Patrick's, Den and Zoe's or Frank and Pat's?

8 Who in *Coronation Street* had a fling with her stepson Jamie?

9 In *EastEnders*, Irene had an affair with which yoga loving toy boy?

10 Which *EastEnder* told his young lover 'This ain't about love, it's about sex'?

Answers on page 218

11 What was the name of the Weatherfield hairdressing rep who two-timed his other half with Candice: Tim, Tom or Tony?

12 Frank Butcher famously turned up on Pat's doorstep wearing nothing but what: a policeman's helmet, a revolving bow tie or a leopardskin thong?

13 Which young *Neighbour* had an affair with his mum's golf partner: Brett Stark, Malcolm Kennedy or Toadfish?

14 Jane Beale had an affair with which member of the Mitchell family?

15 Pat and Frank had an affair away from Walford while on holiday in which country: Portugal, Spain or Italy?

16 Which Summer Bay father had an affair with his son's girlfriend?

17 Alan Jackson had an affair with which Walford singer?

18 Which serial love rat had affairs with Zoe Slater, Michelle Fowler and Kate Morton amongst others?

19 East End market trader Sanjay Kapoor had an affair with his wife Gita's sister. What was her name?

20 *Coronation Street's* Jenny Bradley had a relationship with which floppy-haired Frenchman?

Answers on page 218

Animal Magic

QUIZ 73

1 What was the name of the poodle owned by Den Watts in *EastEnders*?

2 In *Neighbours*, the Kennedy family kept what type of animal in their back garden to act as a lawnmower: sheep, goat or pig?

3 Which *Coronation Street* character is a keen pigeon fancier?

4 Which *Neighbour* died after falling off his horse at the Oakey Rodeo?

5 What animal appears in the opening credits of *Coronation Street*?

6 In *Neighbours*, what was the name of the greyhound owned by Philip Martin and Lou Carpenter: Suede Tess, Leather Tess or Denim Tess?

7 In *Emmerdale*, Sadie King's dog Damon was killed by which character?

8 In *EastEnders*, which character owned a dog called Willy?

9 In *Coronation Street*, Liam's labrador puppy was named after which heavy metal star?

10 Which character in *Neighbours* had a pet snake called Oscar?

Answers on page 218

11 In *Emmerdale*, what is the name of Edna's dog: Bingley, Batley or Bradley?

12 Harold Bishop was arrested at an animal rights demo dressed up as what?

13 A cat in *Neighbours* was named after Elvis Presley's manager. What was his name?

14 Which *Coronation Street* dog was named after a famous footballer?

15 In *EastEnders* what is the name of the Belgian Shepherd dog originally owned by Robbie Jackson and later by Gus Smith?

16 True or false: Grant Mitchell and Nigel Bates owned a greyhound called Freida?

17 Which *Emmerdale* star rode a horse called Valentine?

18 In *EastEnders*, who owned a gerbil called Rolf?

19 In *Coronation Street*, Mavis and Percy both kept which type of bird?

20 Walford battleaxe Mo Harris ended up with what animal when she thought she was buying a Christmas Turkey?

Answers on page 218

Babes

QUIZ 74

1 Which *Hollyoaks* character was voted Sexiest Female at the 2007 British Soap Awards?

2 Which Erinsborough beauty was jilted at the altar by Mark Gottlieb?

3 Which *Coronation Street* brunette was engaged to Sonny Dhillon?

4 The actress who played *Emmerdale's* Tricia Dingle is married to which Liverpool footballer?

5 Isla Fisher played which character in *Home and Away*?

6 Which feisty *Coronation Street* resident got engaged in order to win a bet?

7 Who in *Emmerdale* invented a chatroom girlfriend called Fireblade for her lonely boss?

8 Which *Hollyoaks* brunette went on a reality TV show and revealed that Dan Hunter had lost his virginity to her?

9 In *Neighbours*, who married Brad Willis?

10 Which Mitchell did Mel Healy not have a fling with: Phil, Grant or Billy?

11 Jennifer Ellison played which *Brookside* babe?

12 Which *Hollyoaks* beauty had relationships with Cameron Clark, Jake Dean and an older man called Kristian Hargreaves?

13 Where did Tyrone Dobbs propose to Maria Sutherland?

14 Which *Neighbour* snogged her sister's fiancé Marc Lambert which led to the cancellation of their wedding?

15 Who in *Hollyoaks* had relationships with Dan Hunter, Ben Davies and Tony Hutchinson: Geri Hudson, Izzy Cornwell or Jude Cunningham?

16 Albert Square's Stacey Slater had an affair with which older man?

17 Which former Page Three girl played Carrie Nicholls in *Emmerdale*?

18 What is Erinsborough's Heidi Steiger better known as?

19 Which Weatherfield schoolgirl seduced her teacher John Stape?

20 Which *EastEnders* actress won the Sexiest Female award at the British Soap Awards in 2002, 2003 and 2004?

Answers on page 218

Bad Boys

1 What is the name of Dot Cotton's very naughty son?

2 In *Home and Away*, who abused Dani then later had a relationship with her sister?

3 In *Coronation Street* who stole the deeds to Rita Fairclough's house and then tried to kill her?

4 Which *Emmerdale* bad boy fathered a child with his second cousin?

5 What is the name of the evil twin in *Neighbours*: Cameron Robinson or Robert Robinson?

6 Who regularly tormented and abused Little Mo and on one occasion smashed her face into her Christmas dinner?

7 In *Coronation Street* which gangster killed Tony Horrocks?

8 What was the occupation of *Hollyoaks* bad boy Scott Anderson: footballer, rugby player or singer?

9 In *Emmerdale*, who killed Rachel Hughes by throwing her off a cliff?

10 Which Walford wide boy was wrongly imprisoned for trying to kill Phil Mitchell?

Answers on page 218

11 Which *Brookside* bad boy killed the wife and son of his best friend Terry Sullivan?

12 Richard Hillman framed which unfortunate youngster for the murder of Maxine Peacock?

13 Which *EastEnder* killed his ex, Saskia, after hitting her over the head with an ashtray?

14 Grant Mitchell fled Britain to start a new life in which South American country: Brazil, Argentina or Mexico?

15 Which Weatherfield wrong 'un 'sold' his son Tommy to his parents-in-law the Hortons?

16 Which *EastEnder* raped Kathy Beale?

17 Who in *EastEnders* owned an illegal gambling den called The Market Cellar?

18 Richard Hillman left which *Coronation Street* character for dead after he fell from a bannister?

19 Paul Robinson spent seven years in prison for what crime: fraud, arson or manslaughter?

20 In *EastEnders*, who killed Andy Hunter by pushing him off a motorway bridge?

Answers on page 218

Behind The Bar

1. Boyzone's Keith Duffy played which Rovers Return bar and cellarman?

2. Which sisters are the joint landladies of *Emmerdale's* Woolpack?

3. What is the name of the only bar in Summer Bay: Noah's Bar, Alf's Bar or Hayley's Bar?

4. What is the name of the pub in *Hollyoaks*?

5. Who is the landlord of the pub in *Hollyoaks*?

6. Fred Elliott died on the day he was supposed to marry which Rovers Return manageress?

7. Who was the landlord of The Woolpack alongside Amos Brearley?

8. Which *Coronation Street* barman famously borrowed Mrs Walker's Rover 2000 car then watched it sink into a lake: Jack Duckworth, Fred Gee or Alec Gilroy?

9. Who was the regular cleaner of the Rovers Return from the 1960s to the 1980s?

10. Which member of the Dingle family died when The Woolpack's chimney fell through the roof after being struck by lightning?

11 What was the name of the bar in *Brookside*?

12 Who was the manager of the bar in *Brookside*: Barry Grant, Jacqui Farnham or Jimmy Corkhill?

13 Which of the following hasn't worked behind the bar at the Queen Vic: Tiffany Mitchell, Mel Healy or Teresa di Marco?

14 Shane Ritchie played which popular Queen Vic manager?

15 What was the name of Alan Turner's granddaughter who regularly worked behind the bar at The Woolpack?

16 Which Rovers Return barmaid was the lead singer in Vernon Tomlin's band: Michelle Connor, Leanne Battersby or Violet Wilson?

17 Which Queen Vic barman bedded Carly whilst going out with her stepsister Chelsea?

18 Which Woolpack manager was at one time married to vicar Ashley Thomas?

19 Who were the five characters who died in the fire at the pub in *Hollyoaks*?

20 Rita from *Coronation Street* sometimes sang in which cabaret club: The Gatsby, Hemingway's or Fitzgerald's?

Answers on page 219

Bitches

1 In *EastEnders* how did Janine cause the death of Barry Evans?

2 Which *Dynasty* stirrer was noted for smoking black Nat Sherman Cigarillos?

3 What was the profession of Walford's Stella Crawford?

4 What did Summer Bay teacher Angie Russell hide in order to make Sally look bad in front of the inspectors: her books, her OCD pills or her chalk?

5 Which *Emmerdale* schemer stole some jewellery from a client but let her husband take the rap and go to prison?

6 Whose constant scheming led to the mental breakdown of Erinsborough's Max Hoyland?

7 Which *Hollyoaks* minx had an affair with Kurt Benson, which led to the break up of his marriage?

8 What big lie did *Emmerdale's* Nicola tell Carlos in order to get him to propose: she had won the lottery, she only had six months to live or she was pregnant?

9 Who punched Marlon Dingle at his and Tricia's engagement party then snogged him the night before the wedding?

10 Which Walford wide boy did Janine team up with in order to fleece the hapless Barry?

Answers on page 219

11 Tracy Barlow had a relationship with which former lover of her mum?

12 Izzy Hoyland from *Neighbours* had an affair with Pete Gartside but what was his occupation: footballer, actor or airline pilot?

13 Cindy Beale fled Walford with children Peter and Steven to which country: Italy, Spain or Greece?

14 How did Kim Tate dramatically leave *Emmerdale*: in a helicopter, in a Rolls Royce or in the back of a police van?

15 Which Walford resident punched murderer Chrissie Watts as she tried to leave the country at Stansted Airport?

16 Which *Emmerdale* schemer ruined Charity's wedding to Tom King?

17 Suranne Jones played which Weatherfield drama queen?

18 Who punched *Emmerdale's* Nicola in the face after the scheming blonde had got Miles hopelessly drunk?

19 *Emmerdale* schemer Kim and husband Steve Marchant planned to make some dodgy cash by stealing what: an antique vase, a horse or a diamond?

20 Who did *Hollyoaks* minx Claire Devine kidnap in order to get back at Warren?

Answers on page 219

Blondes

1 Which blonde *EastEnder* had an infamous affair with her husband's brother?

2 Richard Hillman's third *Coronation Street* murder victim was which blonde hairdresser?

3 In *Coronation Street* who left Curly Watts for a career as a beautician in the Far East?

4 In *Emmerdale*, who faked her own death then later poisoned her husband who subsequently died from a heart attack?

5 Which stunning *Neighbour* died in a car crash shortly after marrying Toadfish?

6 In *EastEnders*, Mel Healy dumped which man just minutes after they'd got married?

7 Which blonde was *Emmerdale's* Chris Tate's second wife: Rachel, Ruth or Rebecca?

8 *Hollyoaks* lifeguard Adam Morgan dumped which stunning blonde for which other stunning blonde?

9 Which scheming *EastEnder* arranged for her husband Ian Beale to be shot by a hitman?

10 Which Weatherfield blonde had an affair with Kevin Webster and married Des Barnes?

Answers on page 219

11 Which *Hollyoaks* teacher had an affair with pupil Justin Burton?

12 Annalise Hartman left Ramsay Street to start a new career as what: film director, beautician or dog trainer?

13 In *Neighbours*, Plain Jane Superbrain was the granddaughter of which Ramsay Street gossip?

14 Which Summer Bay drama teacher was sacked for misconduct before marrying millionaire Graham Walters?

15 Zoe Lister plays which blonde stunner in Hollyoaks?

16 Which hairdresser went into a coma after falling from a window trying to escape the *Brookside* siege?

17 Whose blonde beehive was in 2007 voted as The Worst Haircut in soap history?

18 Kathy Bates married which *Emmerdale* heart-throb: Dave Glover, Archie or Phil Pierce?

19 Gemma Atkinson played which character in *Hollyoaks*: Lisa Hunter, Beth Morgan or Ellie Mills?

20 Which *Hollyoaks* regular slept with Brian, the boyfriend of her best friend Zara?

Answers on page 219

Brothers and Sisters

1 Following the death of his parents' who brought up *Hollyoaks'* baby Tom?

2 What were the names of Erinsborough's Alessi twins?

3 In *EastEnders*, what were the names of the four di Marco siblings?

4 In *Coronation Street* what are the names of Jerry Morton's four children?

5 Actors Nick and John Pickard play which pair of *Hollyoaks* characters?

6 In *Neighbours*, what were the names of Jim Robinson's five children?

7 Which *Brookside* pair had an incestuous relationship?

8 What are the names of Karl Kennedy's four children?

9 Twins Peter and Susan are the children of which long term Weatherfield resident?

10 Debs Brownlow was the sister of which Weatherfield landlady?

Answers on page 219

11 How did *Emmerdale's* Skilbeck twins die?

12 When Douglas Potts said 'that woman reeks of smut' he was talking about which *Emmerdale* sister?

13 Which Walford sisters opened up the R&R Club?

14 Who is the eldest of Ramsay Street's Kinski children?

15 *Coronation Street's* Judy Mallett gave birth to twins. What were they called?

16 In *Coronation Street* what was the name of Vikram Desai's sister?

17 Kylie Minogue played Charlene in *Neighbours* but what was the character played by sister Dannii Minogue in *Home and Away*?

18 Kim Appleby of Mel & Kim appeared in which soap?

19 Which McDonald brother kissed a transsexual called Shania?

20 In *Hollyoaks*, what were the names of Gordon Cunningham's five children?

Answers on page 219

Crime

1 Who was the *Hollyoaks* serial killer?

2 What is the name of the gangland organisation in *EastEnders*: The Mob, The Company or The Firm?

3 Why was *Neighbours'* Scott Timmins arrested in 2004?

4 Tracy Barlow killed Charlie Stubbs using what object: an ashtray, a statue or a golf club?

5 Toadfish ended up in a coma thanks to which crooked Erinsborough businessman?

6 Gangster Frazer Henderson had an affair with which *Coronation Street* barmaid: Liz McDonald, Bet Lynch or Natalie Horrocks?

7 Who in *Home and Away* was sent to prison for a fraud that was actually committed by his father?

8 Who returned to *Coronation Street* in 2007 after a lengthy spell behind bars?

9 Who was voted Villain of the Year at the 2007 British Soap Awards: Clare Devine, David Platt or Hayley Lawson?

10 Richard Hillman was disguised as which Weatherfield tearaway when he tried to kill Emily Bishop?

Answers on page 219

11 True or false: *Emmerdale's* Tom King died after being struck by a statue of a dog's head?

12 Which *Hollyoaks* footballer tried to rape Geri Hudson?

13 Dirty Den Watts was shot by a gun hidden in a bunch of what type of flowers?

14 Who almost died after swallowing one of David Platt's ecstasy pills?

15 What was the name of the actor who played *Brookside* wide boy Barry Grant?

16 What was the name of the *EastEnders* gangster Angel's wife: Precious, Honey or Chantelle?

17 Who was the wages clerk killed in bungled robbery at Mike Baldwin's factory?

18 Who when visiting the grave of Steve Owen left flowers saying 'Dear Steve, rot in hell'?

19 Actor Billy Murray played which *EastEnders* mobster?

20 In *Coronation Street*, who kidnapped Ashley and Claire Peacock's son Freddie?

Answers on page 219

Golden Oldies

⭐**1** Jim Branning proposed to Dot at which London landmark?

⭐**2** Which *Coronation Street* veteran is famous for her hot pots?

⭐**3** Who is the longest serving character in *Coronation Street*?

⭐**4** In *EastEnders* what was the name of the eldest member of the Tavernier family: Jules, Jerry or Jethro?

⭐**5** Which *Emmerdale* gossip queen once killed Butch Dingle's pet rat and hit a policeman with a frying pan?

⭐**6** Which blue rinsed pensioner tried and failed to romance Weatherfield pensioner Percy Sugden?

⭐**7** In *Neighbours* what was the name of Jim Robinson's mother-in-law?

⭐**8** Where does Dot Cotton work: the launderette, the bookies or the pub?

⭐**9** Patrick Trueman had an affair with which long time Albert Square resident: Pat, Peggy or Pauline?

⭐**10** In *Neighbours*, what was Mrs Mangel's first name: Betty, Nellie or Enid?

⭐**11** Which Woolpack regular famously had no teeth: Seth Armstrong, Mr Wilkes or Zak Dingle?

Answers on page 220

12 Which *Coronation Street* regular was famous for wearing curlers in her hair?

13 In *Home and Away* Colleen Smart got addicted to what: drinking, gambling or painkillers?

14 In *Coronation Street*, what was the name of Maureen Holdsworth's wheelchair bound mother?

15 Which *Emmerdale* oldie has had dogs called Batley and Tootsie?

16 What job did Percy Sugden take after leaving as caretaker of Weatherfield Community Centre: lollipop man or traffic warden?

17 Which wealthy Weatherfield OAP two-timed Blanche Hunt with her own granddaughter?

18 Mo Harris was sentenced to 100 hours community service for what dodgy activity: selling duty free cigarettes, selling pirate DVDs or bigamy?

19 In *Neighbours*, what was the name of Des Clarke's interfering mother: Eileen, Ethel or Edna?

20 Which *Emmerdale* oldie was famous for his bushy sideburns?

Answers on page 220

Grumpy Old Men

QUIZ 82

1 Who moved in with Ken Barlow after the death of his niece Valerie?

2 What was the name of Dot Cotton's first husband: Charlie, Billy or Eddie?

3 What was the occupation of *Emmerdale's* Seth Armstrong: gamekeeper, innkeeper or lockkeeper?

4 Which grumpy old man was originally caretaker of the Weatherfield Community Centre and was a lodger with Emily Bishop?

5 In *Home and Away* whose sheep were poisoned by Geoff?

6 Which *Coronation Street* lazybones was described in a national newspaper as 'the uncrowned king of the non-working classes'?

7 Who in *Brookside* was married to Edna and was constantly arguing with his lodger Ralph Hardwick?

8 Which nosy gossip works alongside Rita in The Kabin?

9 In *Coronation Street*, Alf Roberts married which owner of the corner shop: Renee, Renata or Rebecca?

10 Who arrived in *Emmerdale* on the day of Butch Dingle's funeral but was so drunk that he fell asleep during the service?

Answers on page 220

11 In *EastEnders*, Michael Elphick played which nasty piece of work?

12 Which job hasn't Joe Scully done: truck driver, builder or barman?

13 In *EastEnders*, what was the name of Tiffany's father: Terry, Tommy or Tony?

14 Who in *Emmerdale* brought a bride back from The Philippines: Eric Pollard, Alan Turner or Mr Wilkes?

15 Which East End taxi driver was rebuffed in his attempts to romance Peggy Mitchell?

16 Which *Coronation Street* curmudgeon was Annie Walker's cellarman and sometime personal chauffeur?

17 Who was twice voted the Mayor of Weatherfield: Percy Sugden, Alf Roberts or Fred Gee?

18 Which Ramsay Street builder had children called Adam, Gaby, Brad and Cody?

19 Which *EastEnder* took the rap for Martin Fowler's marijuana growing activities?

20 In *Neighbours*, what was the name of Gail's mechanic father: Rob Lewis, Richard Lewis or Rodney Lewis?

Answers on page 220

Guest Appearances

1 Which member of the Royal Family has appeared in *Coronation Street*: Prince Charles, The Queen or Prince Phillip?

2 Which former wife of a Beatle made a guest appearance in American soap *Days of Our Lives*?

3 Neil Morrissey appeared in *Neighbours* in 2007. What job did he have in the show: a lawyer, a policeman or a priest?

4 Which Welsh opera singer had a cameo role in *Emmerdale*: Bryn Terfel or Katherine Jenkins?

5 Which madcap comedian made a guest appearance in *Coronation Street* as elderly fitness fanatic Ernie Crabbe?

6 Little Britain's Lou and Andy made a cameo appearance in which show: *Neighbours*, *Home and Away* or *Hollyoaks*?

7 Joanna Lumley has appeared in which soap opera: *EastEnders*, *Emmerdale* or *Coronation Street*?

8 Which Pop Idol wannabe made a cameo appearance in *Hollyoaks* in 2003: Will Young, Gareth Gates or Darius?

9 Which chat show host made a guest appearance in *Neighbours* in 2007?

10 Sir Ian McKellan played which literary con artist in *Coronation Street*?

11 Singer Marti Pellow made a guest appearance in which show?

12 True or false: Little Britain star Matt Lucas has appeared in *EastEnders*?

13 Which Wimbledon winner has been in *Home and Away*: Pat Rafter, Lleyton Hewitt or Andre Agassi?

14 Which comedian played Eric Gartside in *Coronation Street* and went on a couple of dates with Shelly Unwin?

15 Which girl band appeared in *Home and Away* as Whole Again: Sugababes, Spice Girls or Atomic Kitten?

16 Before becoming famous which one of the Spice Girls appeared as an extra in *EastEnders*?

17 True or false: both Peter Stringfellow and Les Dennis appeared in *Family Affairs*?

18 Which legendary cricketer once made a guest appearance in *Neighbours*: Shane Warne, Ian Botham or Andrew Flintoff?

19 Which crooner had a cameo role in *Emmerdale* in 2005: Tom Jones, Tony Christie or Paul Anka?

20 Which member of the Monty Python team has appeared in *Home and Away*: John Cleese, Eric Idle or Michael Palin?

Answers on page 220

Hunks

1 Which *Coronation Street* character was voted Sexiest Male at the 2007 British Soap Awards?

2 Who had relationships with Deirdre Barlow, Geena Gregory, Natalie Horrocks, Maya Sharma and Tracy Barlow?

3 In *Hollyoaks* what is Calvin Valentine's occupation?

4 Which handsome *Emmerdale* barman has a drag queen alter ego called Thelma Louise?

5 In *EastEnders*, Dennis Rickman had a relationship with which Slater sister: Lynne, Kat or Zoe?

6 Summer Bay hunks Kim and Hugh were involved in a love triangle with which psychiatric registrar?

7 Who in *Emmerdale* has dated Del Dingle and Jasmine Thomas and also kissed Katie Sugden?

8 Chris Quentin played which *Coronation Street* heart-throb?

9 In *EastEnders*, who was Beppe di Marco's estranged wife: Sandra, Sarah or Saskia?

10 Who won the Mr Erinsborough contest run by Toadie's shop Bounce?

Answers on page 220

11 Which *Emmerdale* heart-throb was married to Kathy Bates and had an affair with Kim Tate?

12 Which of the following did Steve Owen not have a relationship with: Saskia, Mel or Lisa?

13 Jeff Hordley played which bit of *Emmerdale* rough?

14 What is *Emmerdale's* Andy Sugden's occupation?

15 Matt di Angelo who played Deano Wicks, appeared in which show: *Strictly Come Dancing, I'm A Celebrity Get Me Out Of Here* or *Celebrity Big Brother*?

16 Actor Richard Fleeshman played which Weatherfield heart-throb?

17 In *Neighbours* what was Drew Kirk's home town: Oakey, Hokey or Cokey?

18 Which *Hollyoaks* hunk had relationships with Cindy Cunningham, Lisa Hunter, Izzy Cornwell and Mandy Richardson?

19 Actor Chris Fountain plays which *Hollyoaks* beefcake?

20 What was the name of Walford smoothie David Wicks' handsome yet tormented son?

Answers on page 220

Life After Soaps

QUIZ 85

1 Which *EastEnder* swapped Albert Square for the police beat in Aidensfield, Yorkshire?

2 Which former *Neighbour* starred in the Oscar-winning film *LA Confidential*: Jason Donovan, Guy Pearce or Alan Dale?

3 *Coronation Street's* Amanda Griffin went on to star in which hairdressing drama?

4 Which *EastEnder* hosts a BAFTA award-winning show on gangs: Ross Kemp, Leslie Grantham or Steve McFadden?

5 Suranne Jones starred alongside Ray Winstone in which detective drama: *Vincent, Frost* or *Rebus*?

6 Which former *EastEnder* went on to play the evil Gabriel Kent in *The Bill*?

7 Which former *Neighbour* found fame in America as Bradford Meade in '*Ugly Betty*'?

8 James Redmond aka Finn from *Hollyoaks*, later appeared in which medical drama?

9 Tina Hobley who played Samantha Failsworth in *Coronation Street*, later appeared alongside Nick Berry in what seaside drama?

10 Gary Lucy of *The Bill* previously appeared in which soap: *Hollyoaks, Neighbours* or *Eastenders*?

11 Which Hollywood superstar played Kenny Larkin in *Neighbours*?

12 Gillian Taylforth played the role of Jackie Pascoe-Webb in which football drama: *Dream Team* or *Footballers' Wives*?

13 Which *EastEnder* starred in army drama *Red Cap* and is now treading the boards in the West End?

14 Paul Usher aka *Brookside's* Barry Grant, went on to play which character in *The Bill*?

15 Geoffrey Hughes aka *Coronation Street's* Eddie Yates, played the slobbish Onslow in which BBC comedy?

16 Which former *Neighbour* had a successful comedy career and also hosted *The Big Breakfast*?

17 Peter Martin who played Len Reynolds in *Emmerdale*, also appeared in which comedy series as Joe Carroll?

18 Which *Brookside* star went on to appear in the successful movies *The Land Girls* and *Goal*?

19 *Hollyoaks* star Will Mellor found success in which BBC sitcom?

20 Which *Home and Away* star appeared in the 2005 film *The Wedding Crashers*?

Answers on page 220

Life Before Soaps

QUIZ 86

1 Which star of the *Carry On* films became a regular in *EastEnders*?

2 Which *Worzel Gummidge* and *Give Us A Clue* star played Caroline Bishop in *EastEnders*?

3 Which *EastEnders* star appeared on the Blur song *Parklife*?

4 Kym Ryder who plays Michelle Connor in *Coronation Street*, was a member of which band: Hear'say, Liberty X or Girls Aloud?

5 True or false: Sue Cleaver who plays Eileen Grimshaw in *Coronation Street*, is a trained opera singer?

6 Which *EastEnders* actress starred in the BBC flatshare sitcom *Game On*?

7 Which *Brookside* actor used to be a Pontins Blue Coat: Ricky Tomlinson, Paul Usher or Simon O'Brien?

8 Which *Neighbours* actor was a real life bodybuilder, winning the Mr Natural Victoria contest?

9 Which star of comedy *Duty Free* and vet drama *The Chase* went on to play George Trench in *Coronation Street*?

10 Wendy Richard aka Pauline Fowler played which character in *Are You Being Served?*: Mrs Slocombe, Miss Brahms or Mr Rumbold's secretary?

11 Which *Emmerdale* actress has been married to both Liam Gallagher of Oasis and Jim Kerr of Simple Minds?

12 Stephen Yardley who played Vince Farmer in *Family Affairs*, played which bad boy character in nautical drama *Howards' Way*?

13 Which model, famous for her Campari advert catchphrase of 'Luton Airport', played Steph Stokes in *Emmerdale*?

14 Michael Elphick who played Harry Slater in *EastEnders*, starred in which motorbike-based drama?

15 Martin Kemp who played Steve Owen in *EastEnders* found fame with which pop group: Duran Duran, Spandau Ballet or Haircut 100?

16 Ian Lavender, who played Derek in *EastEnders*, appeared as which character in classic comedy *Dads Army*?

17 Which drum 'n' bass star and *Celebrity Big Brother* contestant played the gangster Angel in *EastEnders*?

18 Comedian Bobby Davro appeared in which soap?

19 Louise Jameson who played Rosa di Marco in *EastEnders*, starred in which 1980s detective series: *Bergerac*, *Hazell* or *Rockliffe's Babies*?

20 Which former Bond girl had a brief spell in *Coronation Street* as Rula Romanoff: Honor Blackman, Ursula Andress or Eunice Gayson?

Answers on page 221

Match The Character

The following characters appeared in which soaps?

1 Alfie Moon

2 Ned Glover

3 Cliff Barnes

4 Sunita Parekh

5 Rick Alessi

6 Fred Fonseca

7 Alf Roberts

8 Jeff Colby

9 Angel Parrish

10 Eddie Banks

11 Ida Clough

12 Mark Gottlieb

13 Amy Turtle

14 Danni Stark

15 David Hunter

16 Eileen Clarke

17 Jules Tavernier

18 Ray Krebbs

19 Bert Tilsley

20 Leonard Kempinski

Answers on page 221

Matriarchs

QUIZ 88

1 In *EastEnders*, what was the name of Pauline Fowler's mother who ruled the family with a rod of iron?

2 In *Coronation Street*, what was the name of Brian Tilsley's interfering mother?

3 Which Albert Square dragon works on the clothes stall in the Bridge Street Market: Mo Harris, Peggy Mitchell or Dot Cotton?

4 In *Neighbours*, what was the name of Charlene and Henry's mum?

5 Which Summer Bay resident was the foster mother of Steven Matheson, Frank Morgan and Carly Morris?

6 Which Ramsay Street matriarch looked after the Robinson family as well as taking in an assortment of waifs and strays?

7 In *EastEnders*, what was the name of Frank Butcher's pestering mother?

8 What is the name of *Coronation Street's* Liz McDonald's only grandchild?

9 What are the names of *Emmerdale* matriarch Viv Hope's four children?

10 At the funeral of which EastEnd matriarch did Pete Beale propose a toast to 'that bloody old bag'?

11 Sheila Mercier played which *Emmerdale* matriarch for over 20 years?

12 In *Neighbours*, what were the names of Pam Willis's four children?

13 Who went from being the town alcoholic to one of its most respected residents, working as a secretary at Summer Bay High?

14 Which Walford matriarch had a relationship with landscape gardener Jack Edwards?

15 In *Coronation Street*, what are the names of Sally's two daughters?

16 Which fearsome Erinsborough mother had children called Brett, Danni, Darren and Louise?

17 Which Walford mother had four children with four different fathers?

18 Whose final words before leaving Erinsborough were 'I don't know what I would have done without you girls': Lyn Scully, Valda Sheergold or Ruth Martin?

19 Nicole Barber-Lane plays which *Hollyoaks* matriarch?

20 Which Weatherfield resident said 'I'm a lady and a lot more as well, as you'd find out if you came to lodge with me'?

Answers on page 221

Medical Matters

1 What was the name of the long serving doctor in *EastEnders*?

2 In *Neighbours*, Dr Karl Kennedy didn't have an affair with which of the following: Izzy Hoyland, Pam Willis or Sarah Beaumont?

3 Which Summer Bay doctor died of cancer of the brain on Valentine's Day 2006?

4 In *Coronation Street*, which one of Gail's husbands was a nurse: Brian Tilsley, Martin Platt or Richard Hillman?

5 Who was the ginger-haired doctor who appeared in *Neighbours* between 1986 and 1989?

6 What is the name of Susan Kennedy's doctor nephew?

7 Nurse Naomi Julien had a steamy lesbian kiss with which character in *EastEnders*?

8 Which Walford doctor proposed to Little Mo?

9 In *EastEnders*, which doctor dated both Kat and Zoe Slater?

10 True or false: Lesley Johnston, who played sinister Laura Burns in *Hollyoaks*, quit acting to become a midwife?

Answers on page 221

11 In *Emmerdale*, Dr Forsythe killed blackmailer Terence Turner with what object: fire extinguisher, candlestick or lead piping?

12 *Coronation Street* doctor Matt Ramsden had an affair with which neighbour?

13 How did nurse Dee Bliss meet her end: car crash, plane crash or horse riding accident?

14 In *EastEnders*, who replaced Dr Legg on his retirement?

15 Which Scottish male nurse died in Walford after being knocked down by a lorry?

16 In *Coronation Street*, who donated a kidney to save the life of her dying grandson?

17 Which of the Scully sisters had a battle with cancer: Steph, Flick or Michelle?

18 In *Coronation Street*, who had an affair with nurse Rebecca Hopkins?

19 In *EastEnders*, who was arrested for attempting to steal Dawn's baby?

20 Which of Dr Karl Kennedy's on screen children now plays a doctor in the American drama *House*?

Answers on page 221

Merry Christmas

1 Which *EastEnder* smashed up his house after admitting to stealing money from the Christmas club?

2 Dev Alahan had an unlikely Christmas Day romp with which *Coronation Street* resident?

3 Which *Emmerdale* businessman was murdered on Christmas Day 2006?

4 Which of Cindy Beale's children was born on Boxing Day 1989?

5 Which *Coronation Street* bad boy was born on Christmas Day 1990?

6 In *EastEnders*, who did Sharon Watts marry on Boxing Day 1991?

7 *Emmerdale's* Ray Mullan died on Christmas Day 2002 after a confrontation with which man eater?

8 Steve Owen married Mel Healy despite finding out that she'd slept with who on Christmas Day 2000?

9 Which member of the McDonald family dumped his wife on Christmas Day 2004: Andy, Jim or Steve?

10 Who gave birth to a son called Liam in the Queen Vic on Christmas Day 1998?

Answers on page 221

11 Who did *Coronation Street's* Ashley Peacock marry on Christmas Day 2005?

12 Which Walford villain stabbed Dennis Rickman to death on New Year's Eve 2005?

13 Weatherfield mischief maker David Platt ruined his family's Christmas after discovering whose diary?

14 Who stopped Walford footballer Aidan Brosnan from jumping to his death from a tower block on Christmas Day 1992?

15 Which *Emmerdale* postmaster was shot dead on Christmas Day 1998?

16 Which Walford taxi driver knocked over and killed a young pedestrian while over the limit on Christmas Eve 1992?

17 Weatherfield's Rosie Webster was born on Christmas Eve in which unlikely location: The Rovers, Don Brennan's taxi or The Kabin?

18 *Emmerdale's* Dave Glover died on Boxing Day 1996 rescuing whose baby: Kim's, Kathy's or Viv's?

19 Which *Coronation Street* resident found out that he had a child called Holly on Christmas Day 2006?

20 Which EastEnd tough was arrested on Boxing Day 1998, for the attempted murder of Tiffany but was later released?

Answers on page 221

More Than One Soap

1 Ross Kemp is best known for playing Grant Mitchell but who did he play in *Emmerdale*?

2 The actor who played which long term Weatherfield resident previously played Cliff Leyton in *Crossroads*?

3 Before appearing in *Coronation Street*, Sue Nicholls made her TV debut as Marilyn Gates on which soap?

4 Emily Symons is best known for playing Marilyn in *Home and Away* and which *Emmerdale* man eater?

5 The actor who played Warren in *EastEnders* is better known for playing which *Hollyoaks* chancer?

6 Which *EastEnders* actress briefly played Dawn in *Brookside*?

7 Gemma Bissix who played the evil Clare Devine in *Hollyoaks*, appeared as which character in *EastEnders*?

8 Which actress played Fran Pearson in *Brookside*, Jo Steadman in *Emmerdale* and Jacqui Hudson in *Hollyoaks*?

9 Sue Jenkins who played Jackie Corkhill in *Brookside*, also played which *Coronation Street* barmaid?

10 Jill Halfpenny played Kate Mitchell in *EastEnders* and which Weatherfield nurse?

Answers on page 222

11 Benjamin Hart who played Adam Rhodes in *Neighbours*, also played which character in Hollyoaks?

12 The actor who played Dr Forrest in *The Young Doctors* is best known for portraying which character in *Neighbours*?

13 Actress Michelle Holmes who played Britt Woods in *Emmerdale* previously appeared as which *Coronation Street* barmaid?

14 Malandra Burrows who played Kathy in *Emmerdale* also appeared in which soap as Lisa Morrissey?

15 Steven Pinder went from playing Roy Lambert in *Crossroads* to which *Brookside* love rat?

16 Christian Ealey played the same character in both *Brookside* and *Hollyoaks* but what was his name?

17 Anne Charleston who played Madge in *Neighbours*, plays which character in *Emmerdale*?

18 Before playing Carrie in *Emmerdale*, Linda Lusardi appeared as Frankie in which soap?

19 Which actor played Peter Phelan in *Brookside*, Gary Adams in *Coronation Street* and Carrie's long lost love Nick in *Emmerdale*?

20 Which soap wasn't created by Phil Redmond: *Brookside*, *Hollyoaks* or *EastEnders*?

Answers on page 222

Nicknames

What were the nicknames of the following characters?

1 Timothy O'Leary

2 Norman Watts

3 Jarrod Rebecchi

4 George Holloway

5 James Bolton

6 David Burke

7 Peter O'Neale

8 Kevin Rebecchi

9 David Crosbie

10 Geoffrey Nugent

11 Libby Fox

12 Richard Cole

13 Sam O'Brien

14 Jane Harris

15 Hannah Martin

16 Thomas Sweeney

17 Simon Wicks

18 Den Watts

19 Brian Fowler

20 Sean Tully

Answers on page 222

Occupations

Match the person with their job.

1	Archie Shuttleworth	**a**	Bookmaker
2	Paddy Kirk	**b**	Hairdresser
3	Sinbad	**c**	Bank manager
4	Des Barnes	**d**	Newsagent
5	Marlon Dingle	**e**	Lawyer
6	Ricky Butcher	**f**	Undertaker
7	Max Farnham	**g**	Taxi driver
8	Donald Fisher	**h**	Car mechanic
9	Audrey Roberts	**i**	Cleaner
10	Philip Martin	**j**	Quantity surveyor
11	Rita Sullivan	**k**	Window cleaner
12	Ashley Thomas	**l**	Doctor
13	Fred Elliott	**m**	Farmer
14	Toadfish Rebecchi	**n**	Market trader
15	Charlie Slater	**o**	Lollipop man
16	Hilda Ogden	**p**	Vet
17	Clive Gibbons	**q**	Chef
18	Jack Sugden	**r**	Butcher
19	Pete Beale	**s**	Vicar
20	Percy Sugden	**t**	School teacher

Answers on page 222

Parents

QUIZ 94

1 In *Coronation Street* who did Tracy Barlow con into thinking that he was the father of young Amy?

2 What is the name of *Emmerdale* rogue Eric Pollard's hunky son?

3 Who was the father of Simon Wicks in *EastEnders*?

4 Dirty Den Watts fathered a child with which teenage mum?

5 Weatherfield veteran Betty Turpin's illegitimate son Gordon Clegg was played by which West End theatre impresario?

6 True or false: Dave Glover fathered Kim Tate's son James?

7 *Coronation Street's* Kevin Webster has fathered three children. Can you name them?

8 Which young *Hollyoaks* resident gave birth to a daughter called Holly?

9 In *EastEnders*, what was the name of Barry and Natalie's son?

10 Which Erinsborough resident went into labour after being locked in a barn at the Oakey Rodeo?

11 In *Neighbours*, what was the name of Des and Daphne's son?

12 Who is the father of *Coronation Street's* Bethany Platt?

13 Which Summer Bay resident gave birth to Pippa Saunders in 2004?

14 Ray Langton is the father of which Weatherfield drama queen?

15 What was the name of Alice and Sam Dingle's son in *Emmerdale*?

16 In *Hollyoaks*, who was the father of Anna Green's son Charlie: Alex, Sam or Max?

17 What are the names of Grant Mitchell's two children?

18 Which Walford mechanic originally thought that he was Bobby Beale's father?

19 Harry and son Dan Mason run which *Coronation Street* establishment?

20 In *Home and Away*, what was the name of Donald and Marilyn Fisher's son: Bobby, Brian or Byron?

Answers on page 222

Quotations

QUIZ 95

1 'Cor, stinks in here' were the first words spoken in which soap?

2 Who told *Coronation Street's* Sean Tully to 'lie back and think of England. Playing Portugal' while trying to seduce him?

3 Which *Neighbour* rapped 'I'm in the House, of the Coffee shop where the food is Grouse'?

4 Who said 'Mike Baldwin is like a vampire, drawing the life out of people, destroying lives': Don Brennan, Steve McDonald or Ken Barlow?

5 Alf Stewart is famous for using which phrase: 'flaming galah', 'flaming kangaroo' or 'flaming koala'?

6 Who spoke the first ever line in *EastEnders*?

7 'You want to bring up Chloe? You couldn't bring up phlegm'. Which Walford matriarch was Sonia talking to?

8 'If you were stood at the end of a cliff all I would say is jump'. Which Weatherfield woman didn't approve of her brother's behaviour?

9 Which *Hollyoaks* minx said 'I've got your sister and if you want to see her alive again you've got to kill Justin'?

10 'Well I may be a toerag but at least I don't pee my pants'. Which Dingle was talking to Laurel as her waters broke?

Answers on page 222

11 Who said 'Tracy Barlow! I mean, even her initials are a killer disease!': Eileen Grimshaw, Karen McDonald or Janice Battersby?

12 'I'd rather burn in hell than take a drink from you.' Peggy Mitchell was unimpressed with the offer of a drink from which Walford gangster?

13 Which *Coronation Street* character was described by Ken Barlow as 'the debonair dynamo of denim'?

14 Which Walford stalwart did Roy Evans describe as 'once a tart always a tart'?

15 Who in *Emmerdale* did Val Lambert describe as having '65 years on the clock, and not a friend in the world'?

16 Which Weatherfield bad boy did Gail describe as 'Norman Bates with a briefcase'?

17 'Ello princess' was regularly said by which EastEnd rogue?

18 Which *Coronation Street* regular is famous for the phrase 'so it is'?

19 In *Hollyoaks* which member of the Morgan family did Dannii Carbone describe as 'being able to start an argument in an empty room': Zara, Beth or Luke?

20 Which long serving Albert Square resident said of herself 'I'm not a sex bomb. I'm a respectable married woman': Dot Cotton, Sharon Watts or Kat Slater?

Answers on page 222

Reality TV

1 Which *Brookside* actress was runner-up in the first series of *Celebrity Big Brother*?

2 Julie Goodyear, Ken Morley and Mikyla Dodd all appeared on which reality show?

3 Bruce Jones, who is better known as Les Battersby, appeared as which legendary crooner on *Celebrity Stars in Their Eyes*?

4 Which *Hollyoaks* star won *Comic Relief Does Fame Academy*: Will Mellor, Jeremy Edwards or Joanna Taylor?

5 *EastEnders* actor John Bardon duetted with which soul diva on *Comic Relief Does Fame Academy*?

6 *Coronation Street's* Tommy Craig appeared for a celebrity team in which football show?

7 Which *Neighbours* actress fractured a rib after a helicopter jump went wrong on *I'm a Celebrity Get Me Out of Here*?

8 Philip Olivier, Michelle Gayle and Terri Dwyer all appeared in which reality show?

9 Letitia Dean and which other *EastEnder* appeared in the 2007 series of *Strictly Come Dancing*?

10 *Coronation Street's* Michael Le Vell won what competition: *Showbiz Snooker*, *Showbiz Poker* or *Showbiz Darts*?

11 What do Sheree Murphy, Sid Owen and Jason Donovan have in common?

12 Which EastEnd landlady traced her family tree on *Who Do You Think You Are*?

13 Which *EastEnders* actress won *Celebrity Masterchef* in 2007: Nadia Sawalha, Pam St Clement or Wendy Richard?

14 *Coronation Street's* Anthony Cotton won which TV singing contest?

15 Which *EastEnder* partnered Anton Du Beke in the 2005 series of *Strictly Come Dancing*: Patsy Palmer, Martine McCutcheon or Daniella Westbrook?

16 *Emmerdale's* Amy Nuttall appeared in which show: *Celebrity Spider Bait*, *Celebrity Snake Bait* or *Celebrity Shark Bait*?

17 Which *EastEnder* won *Celebrity Mastermind* answering questions on Norman Wisdom?

18 *Hollyoaks* stars Paul Danan and Lee Otway and *EastEnder* Michael Greco all appeared in which show?

19 Which *Coronation Street* actor suffered two black eyes after a diving accident in *The Games*?

20 *EastEnders* star Shaun Williamson aka Barry appeared as which rock singer on *Celebrity Stars in Their Eyes*?

Answers on page 223

Singing Soap Stars

1 Which *Neighbour* had a number one hit with *I Should Be So Lucky*?

2 True or false: Boyzone's Shane Lynch starred in *EastEnders*?

3 *Perfect Moment* was a hit for which former *EastEnder*?

4 *Coronation Street's* Suranne Jones appeared as which Material Girl in *Celebrity Stars in Their Eyes*?

5 *Don't It Make You Feel Good* was a hit for which *Neighbour*?

6 True or false: Kevin Kennedy aka Curly Watts played in a band called the *Paris Valentinos* alongside Johnny Marr of *The Smiths*?

7 Which drum 'n' bass star appeared in *EastEnders* as Angel?

8 Who composed the theme tunes to *Emmerdale Farm*, *Neighbours* and *Crossroads*?

9 Which member of Take That was once spotted having a pint in the Queen Vic in *EastEnders*?

10 Anita Dobson aka Angie from *EastEnders* is married to which legendary rock guitarist: Slash, Francis Rossi or Brian May?

Answers on page 223

11 *Every Loser Wins* was a hit for which *EastEnders* heart-throb?

12 Dannii Minogue appeared in which soap: *Neighbours* or *Home and Away*?

13 Which Spandau Ballet star played Steve Owen in *EastEnders*: Gary Kemp, Martin Kemp or Tony Hadley?

14 What was the name of the *Emmerdale* band which had a hit with *Hillbilly Rock*?

15 William Roache aka Ken Barlow sang as which crooner on *Celebrity Stars in Their Eyes*: Perry Como, Frank Sinatra or Dean Martin?

16 Which former *EastEnder* had hits with *Looking Up* and *Sweetness*?

17 Which *Hollyoaks* star appeared as Richard Marx in *Celebrity Stars in Their Eyes*?

18 Delta Goodrem played which character in *Neighbours*?

19 Craig McLachlan had a hit with: *Mona*, *Rhona* or *Fiona*?

20 What was the name of Letitia Dean and Paul Medford's 1986 Top 20 hit?

Answers on page 223

Spin Offs and Specials

1 A series of *Coronation Street* specials featuring the McDonald family was set in which seaside town?

2 *Damon and Debbie* was a spin off from which show?

3 True or false: the cast of *Coronation Street* appeared in a one hour pantomime special in 2005?

4 The one off special *Civvy Street* featured the wartime experiences of the characters from which soap: *Coronation Street*, *EastEnders* or *Emmerdale*?

5 Which *Coronation Street* pair spent their honeymoon on the QE2?

6 Who was the unexpected entertainment manager on the *Coronation Street* QE2 special: Alec Gilroy, Fred Gee or Jack Duckworth?

7 The Dingles met long lost relative Crocodile Dingle in a special set in which country: America, Australia or New Zealand?

8 Which soap produced an x-rated special called *The Lost Weekend*?

9 Steve McDonald tried to stop whose wedding in the *Coronation Street* special *The Brighton Bubble*?

10 Which legendary singer made a surprise guest appearance in *Damon and Debbie*: Morrissey, Boy George or George Michael?

Answers on page 223

11 The 1960s comedy which followed the fortunes of Leonard Swindley was called *Pardon The...*: Smell, Noise or Expression?

12 *Hollyoaks: In The City* followed the exploits of which pair of lovers?

13 True or false: Joan Collins made a special guest appearance in the *Coronation Street* special *Viva Las Vegas*?

14 An *EastEnders* special called *The Naked Truth* centred on the often very bad behaviour of which family: The Mitchells, The Wicks or The Slaters?

15 *Knots Landing* was a spin off of which American favourite?

16 Which couple tied the knot for the second time in *Coronation Street Viva Las Vegas*?

17 A 2001 *Emmerdale* special featured the Dingles in what romantic location: Venice, Paris or Rome?

18 An *EastEnders* special called *In Detention* featured the exploits of which family: The Slaters, The Mitchells or The Fowlers?

19 What was the name of the *Dynasty* spin off: *The Colbys*, *The Carringtons* or *The Jamesons*?

20 Which two long-serving cast members were the team captains on the BBC quiz *A Question Of EastEnders*?

Answers on page 223

Wedding Bells

QUIZ **99**

1 Which Australian pair got married to the song *Suddenly* by Angry Anderson?

2 Which EastEnd wedding was called off after the groom's son revealed that the psycho bride had been bullying him?

3 Which *Emmerdale* schemer sabotaged Tom King and Charity Dingle's wedding by producing photos of the bride snogging another man?

4 Who died at the reception to Ken and Deirdre Barlow's second wedding: Alf Roberts, Mike Baldwin or Ray Langton?

5 Who did Lou Carpenter marry at Her Majesty's Theatre in Melbourne: Trixie, Cheryl or Valda?

6 Which *Coronation Street* barmaid said 'no' when the vicar asked her if she'd take Charlie Stubbs to be her husband?

7 Who punched Beppe di Marco just before Gary Hobbs and Lynne Slater got married: Mo Slater, Kat Slater or Charlie Slater?

8 Which Slater sister's dream of a Christmas white wedding came true when the groom's cousin covered Albert Square with fake snow from a machine?

9 Which pair of *Coronation Street* wasters only got married so they could get some presents?

10 In *EastEnders*, why did Mel leave Ian Beale moments after they'd tied the knot?

11 Which *Neighbour* was kidnapped on her wedding day by an armed robber wearing a gorilla suit: Daphne Clarke, Annalise Hartman or Dee Bliss?

12 Where did Roy and Hayley Cropper get married: The Rovers, St Mary's Church or Roy's Rolls?

13 Which *Emmerdale* groom decided to have his vasectomy reversed on his stag night and was kidnapped by his ex-wife on his wedding day?

14 Which *Neighbour* walked down the aisle wearing a kilt: Drew Kirk, Harold Bishop or Jim Robinson?

15 What unlikely song did *Coronation Street's* Norris play as Ashley and Claire walked down the aisle?

16 In *Neighbours*, Ringo Brown went into a coma after being involved in a minibus crash after whose wedding?

17 Whose stag party had just ended in the first ever episode of *Neighbours*: Des Clarke's, Paul Robinson's or Shane Ramsay's?

18 Where in Summer Bay did Sally and Flynn finally get married: The Diner, the beach or the hospital?

19 In *Coronation Street*, who tried to disrupt Sarah-Louise and Jason's marriage by staging a fake suicide?

20 In *Hollyoaks*, who jilted Tony on their wedding day: Julie, Jenny or Izzy?

Answers on page 223

QUIZ 100

Weren't They in The Bill?

Many actors have made the move from soap opera to Sun Hill. Can you match the character in the soap with the character played by the same actor in *The Bill*? For example Mark Fowler and Gabriel Kent.

1 Barry Grant

2 Irene Raymond

3 Mike Swann

4 Jack Branning

5 Len Harker

6 Luke Morgan

7 Matthew Jackson

8 Kathy Beale

9 Ruby Allen

10 Andy Hunter

11 Johnny Allen

12 Natalie Evans

13 Joel Samuels

14 Gary Bolton

15 Eve Elliott

16 Dr Matt Ramsden

17 Leanne Battersby

18 Diane Murray

19 Dr Marc Eliot

20 Michael Rose

Answers on page 223

a PC Eddie Santini

b PC Cameron Tait

c PC Will Fletcher

d WPC Laura Bryant

e PC Jim Carver

f PC Beth Green

g PC Mike Jarvis

h DI Frank Burnside

i DS Don Beech

j Superintendent Tom Chandler

k PC Des Taviner

l WPC Gemma Osborne

m DS Phil Hunter

n WPC Sheelagh Murphy

o PC Steve Loxton

p Inspector Gina Gold

q DC Ken Drummond

r DC Stevie Moss

s Sergeant Nikki Wright

t DC Terry Perkins

Answers on page 223

QUIZ 1 Page 6

Coronation Street The Early Years Answers
1 The Glad Tidings 2 Tatlock 3 Sunny Jim 4 She was run over by a bus 5 Martha Longhurst 6 Peter Noone 7 Elsie Tanner 8 True 9 Ena Sharples, Minnie Caldwell and Martha Longhurst 10 Annie Walker 11 He was crushed by Len Fairclough's van 12 Policeman 13 Milk stout 14 Jamaica 15 Mavis Riley 16 Miami Modes 17 Lucille Hewitt 18 Renee Bradshaw 19 A scene of Alpine mountains 20 Holland

QUIZ 2 Page 8

Coronation Street The 1980s Answers
1 Eddie Yeats 2 Eunice 3 Sharon Gaskell 4 Victor Pendlebury 5 Emily Bishop 6 Portugal 7 Brian Tilsley 8 Jack Duckworth 9 Rita Fairclough 10 Roman Catholic 11 Percy Sugden 12 Deirdre Barlow 13 Mike Baldwin 14 Through The Kabin letterbox 15 Chalkie Whiteley 16 Jenny 17 Shirley Armitage 18 Paperboy 19 They were all bin men 20 Milkman

QUIZ 3 Page 10

Coronation Street The 1990s Answers
1 Hairdresser 2 Tracy Barlow 3 Handel 4 Norris Cole 5 Rita 6 Spider Nugent 7 Morocco 8 Golden Years 9 Des Barnes 10 Leanne and Nicky Tilsley 11 The Friends of Weatherfield Hospital 12 Ashley Peacock 13 Steve 14 Brendan Scott 15 Fiona Middleton 16 Jack Duckworth and Nicky Tilsley 17 True 18 The Etheric Foundation 19 Airline pilot 20 Steve McDonald

QUIZ 4 Page 12

Coronation Street The Modern Era Answers
1 Cilla Battersby Brown 2 Lindsey 3 An unexploded bomb 4 Bugsy Malone 5 Steve McDonald 6 David Platt 7 Car crash 8 Katya 9 Her brother Paul 10 Lauren 11 Roy and Hayley Cropper's 12 Doreen 13 Blanche Hunt 14 John Stape 15 Casey 16 The Lake District 17 David Platt 18 Darryl Morton's 19 Beverley Callard 20 Mozambique

QUIZ 5 Page 14

Around Weatherfield Answers
1 Valandro's 2 False – it's Streetcars 3 The Kabin 4 Derek Wilton 5 Roy's Rolls 6 Baker 7 True 8 Bessie Street 9 Bettabuys 10 Brian Tilsley 11 County 12 Danny and Sally 13 Underworld 14 Weatherfield General Hospital 15 The Recorder 16 Alf Roberts 17 Ena Sharples 18 Oakhill 19 MVB Motors – short for Michael Vernon Baldwin 20 Wong's

QUIZ 6

Page 16

The Women of Coronation Street Answers
1 Audrey Roberts **2** Bet Lynch **3** Ray Langton, Ken Barlow and Samir Rachid **4** Shirley Armitage **5** Emily Bishop **6** 1960s **7** Hilda Ogden **8** Elsie Tanner **9** Mavis Riley **10** Patterson **11** Exotic dancer **12** Violet Wilson **13** Bobby **14** Sally Seddon **15** Michelle Connor **16** Sally Webster **17** Samantha Failsworth **18** Hilda Ogden **19** Candice Stowe **20** Sue Nicholls who plays Audrey

QUIZ 7

Page 18

Coronation Street Deaths Answers
1 A hairdryer **2** Emily Bishop's husband Ernest was killed **3** He was knocked over by a Blackpool tram **4** Ray Langton **5** He drowned in his car **6** Les Battersby **7** Brian Tilsley **8** Katy Harris **9** Tony Horrocks **10** Drive **11** Don Brennan **12** Jez Quigley **13** Janet Barlow **14** Cancer **15** Fred Elliott **16** Derek Wilton **17** Dean Sykes **18** Anne Malone **19** Ted Sullivan **20** Hit over the head with a crowbar

QUIZ 8

Page 20

Mike Baldwin Answers
1 London **2** Four **3** Ken Barlow **4** Three **5** Vernon **6** Jackie Ingram **7** Mark, Adam and Danny **8** Hilda Ogden **9** The Graffiti Club **10** Gail **11** The Western Front **12** Audrey Roberts **13** Don Brennan's **14** Jim McDonald **15** Alma Sedgwick **16** Angie Freeman **17** Linda **18** Alzheimer's **19** Frankie **20** Johnny Briggs

QUIZ 9

Page 22

Ken Barlow Answers
1 Four **2** True **3** Peter and Susan **4** Valerie Tatlock **5** Mike Baldwin **6** Janet **7** Audrey Roberts **8** True – Ray Langton was Tracy's natural father **9** David **10** Lollipop man **11** True **12** Prince Charles and Lady Diana **13** Albert Tatlock **14** Wendy Crozier **15** 27 **16** Aiden Critchley **17** Adam **18** Denise Osbourne **19** Mike Baldwin **20** Prince Charles and Camilla

QUIZ 10

Page 24

The Battersbys Answers
1 Chesney **2** Nick Tilsley **3** Cocaine **4** A deep fat fryer **5** Italian **6** Dennis Stringer **7** Property developer **8** Maria Sutherland **9** Roger Stiles **10** Greg **11** Kelly Crabtree **12** Janice's **13** Danny Baldwin **14** Status Quo **15** Sam Kingston **16** Paul Connor **17** Las Vegas **18** It was part of a campaign to save Norwegian prawns **19** Paul Clayton **20** It crashed through the ceiling

QUIZ 11
Page 26

The Duckworths Answers
1 Terry 2 Pigeons 3 Golden 4 They added stone cladding 5 Ivy
6 Las Vegas 7 Bet Lynch 8 A stuffed pigeon 9 The Malletts 10 Jack
11 Bin man 12 Kevin Webster 13 Fred Gee 14 Paul, Tommy and
Brad 15 Her knickers were hoisted up a flagpole 16 Bingo hall
17 Betty's Hotshot 18 Joss Shackleton 19 Liz Dawn 20 Bill Tarmey

QUIZ 12
Page 28

The Grimshaws Answers
1 Sarah-Louise Platt 2 Taxi controller 3 Nick Tilsley 4 Dennis Stringer
5 Jason 6 Malta 7 Candice Stowe 8 Karl Foster 9 Ed Jackson
10 True 11 Charlie Stubbs 12 True 13 11 14 London 15 Builder
16 Harry Flagg 17 Phil Nail 18 Ryan Thomas 19 Pat Stanway
20 Todd

QUIZ 13
Page 30

The McDonalds Answers
1 Karen Phillips 2 Vernon Tomlin 3 Soldier 4 Colin Barnes 5 Vicky
6 True 7 Sally Webster 8 Gambling 9 Jez Quigley 10 Katie
11 Perverting the course of justice 12 A fall from scaffolding
13 Derek 14 Spain 15 Blackpool 16 Plumber 17 True 18 Mike
Baldwin 19 Vikram Desai 20 Ronnie Clayton

QUIZ 14
Page 32

The Platts Answers
1 Three 2 Charlie Stubbs 3 Violet Wilson 4 Potter 5 Katy Harris 6 13
7 Three 8 He messed with the brakes on Martin's car 9 Colin Jackson
10 Loosened bolts on some scaffolding 11 Aiden Critchley 12 Canada
13 David Platt 14 Bethany 15 Liverpool 16 It was burnt on Bonfire
Night 17 Phil Nail 18 Billy 19 Tina O'Brien 20 Helen Worth

QUIZ 15
Page 34

Rovers Return Answers
1 Liz McDonald 2 Ken Barlow 3 Hot pot 4 Newton and Ridley
5 Rosamund Street 6 Jack 7 Betty Turpin 8 Billy Walker 9 True
10 The Graffiti Club 11 The Golden Lion 12 Kevin Webster
13 Duggie Ferguson 14 Jack and Vera Duckworth 15 Vicki
16 Shelly Unwin 17 Vernon Tomlin 18 Natalie Barnes – husband
Des was killed 19 True 20 Fred Elliott and Mike Baldwin

QUIZ 16
Page 36

Doctors Answers
1 The Mill Health Centre 2 Letherbridge 3 Nick West 4 Brazil
5 Bracken 6 Buying shoes online 7 Obsessive-Compulsive Disorder
8 Michelle Corrigan 9 Solicitor 10 Breaking patient confidentiality
11 At Greg's wedding 12 Vivien March 13 Christopher Timothy
14 Giving a potassium chloride injection instead of insulin 15 Dr Jude
Carlyle 16 Sadie 17 Dr Ben Kwarme 18 Prince Charles 19 Ronnie
20 Dr Marc Eliot

QUIZ 17
Page 38

EastEnders The Early Years Answers
1 Kenny 2 Reg Cox 3 Nurse 4 Colin Russell and Barry Clark 5 Country
and Western 6 Traffic warden 7 Ali Osman 8 Ethel Skinner 9 Sharon
10 Cot death 11 Donna 12 Mehmet 13 Rod the roadie 14 Sharon
Watts 15 Venice 16 Sparrow 17 Mary Smith 18 The Karims
19 Arthur Fowler 20 Hairdressers

QUIZ 18
Page 40

EastEnders The 1990s Answers
1 Ian Beale 2 Ricky Butcher and Sam Mitchell 3 Steve Elliot 4 Eddie
Royle 5 Prostitute 6 Tricky Dicky 7 Auntie Nelly 8 Saskia 9 Aidan
Brosnan 10 Grant 11 Diane Butcher 12 Beppe 13 Gita 14 Market
inspector 15 Debbie 16 Conor 17 Vanessa Carlton 18 David Wicks
19 Danny Taurus 20 Tiffany's brother Simon

QUIZ 19
Page 42

EastEnders The Modern Era Answers
1 Max Branning 2 Ben Mitchell 3 Li Chong 4 He's not really their
father 5 Stacey and Tanya 6 A champagne bottle and a bow tie
7 Garry Hobbs 8 False – it was a sheep 9 His son Steven 10 Monique
11 Honey 12 Ibiza 13 Jase 14 Tenerife 15 Stacey Slater 16 Steven
Beale 17 Rainie 18 Chelsea and Deano 19 He triggered his nut
allergy 20 A potato from the exhaust of Phil Mitchell's car

QUIZ 20
Page 44

Around Walford Answers
1 Albert Square 2 Bridge Street 3 The Dagmar 4 Ozcabs 5 E20
6 Arthur Fowler 7 The Arches 8 Johnny Allen 9 Deals On Wheels
10 Mr Papadopoulos 11 Romantic Relations 12 Kathy 13 Beale's
Plaice 14 A nail bar 15 Giuseppe's 16 Frank and Pat Butcher
17 Argee Bhajee 18 Sharon 19 The Meal Machine 20 Walford East

QUIZ 21
Page 46

Ian Beale Answers
1 Pete and Kathy 2 Four times 3 Peter and Bobby 4 Ben 5 Lucy
6 Mel Healy 7 He lied about his daughter having fatal cancer 8 Laura
9 True 10 Selling candy floss at Walford Fairground 11 Simon Wicks
12 True 13 Beale's Plaice 14 Janine Butcher 15 She fell down the
stairs 16 Cindy 17 Albert 18 Wellard 19 Grant 20 Adam Woodyatt

QUIZ 22
Page 48

Dot and Jim Branning Answers
1 Charlie 2 The Launderette 3 St Valentine's Day 4 Ethel Skinner
5 Nick 6 False 7 The Queen Vic 8 Carol 9 Ashley 10 Nigel
11 Shoplifting 12 Her bingo winnings 13 Sonia Fowler 14 Mark
Fowler's 15 Rebecca 16 True 17 Fake charity collector 18 Tomas
19 June Brown 20 John Bardon

QUIZ 23
Page 50

Pat Butcher Answers
1 Pete Beale 2 Simon and David 3 A bookmakers 4 True
5 Charlie Slater 6 Frank Butcher 7 Janine 8 Drink driving 9 Stephen
10 PatCabs 11 Andy Hunter 12 Peggy 13 Roy Evans 14 Barry Evans
15 True 16 Sharon 17 Roy Evans 18 Joan 19 Harris 20 Pam St
Clement

QUIZ 24
Page 52

The Queen Vic Answers
1 Den Watts handed them to Angie 2 Red 3 Alfie Moon 4 Pete Beale
5 Pauline Fowler 6 Pat 7 Tiffany 8 Grant Mitchell 9 Den Watts
10 Eddie Royle 11 Jan 12 The Dagmar 13 James Willmott-Brown
14 Jim Branning 15 Phil Mitchell 16 Michelle Fowler 17 A dog-
shaped doorstop 18 Tracy 19 Chrissie 20 Harry Slater

QUIZ 25
Page 54

The Fowlers Answers
1 Den Watts 2 16 3 Lofty Holloway 4 The fruit and veg stall
5 Nick Cotton 6 USA 7 Jamie Mitchell 8 Salsa dancing class 9 Ruth
10 Geoff Barnes 11 Willy Roper 12 Grant Mitchell 13 Christine
Hewitt 14 HIV 15 Spencer Moon 16 Lisa 17 Jeff Healy 18 Sarah
Cairns 19 Martin 20 Gill

QUIZ 26
Page 56

The Mitchells Answers

1 Grant, Phil and Sam **2** Harry Slater **3** Kate **4** The Paras **5** George Palmer **6** Kathy **7** Frank Butcher **8** Ricky Butcher and Andy Hunter **9** Martin Fowler **10** Courtney **11** Billy **12** Lisa **13** Carla **14** Beppe **15** Nadia Borovac **16** Grant Mitchell **17** Roxy and Ronnie Mitchell **18** Lorna **19** Phil Mitchell **20** Louise – she was Tiffany's mum

QUIZ 27
Page 58

The Slaters Answers

1 Taxi driver **2** Harry **3** Zoe **4** Sonia Jackson's **5** He proposed using alphabet spaghetti **6** Mo **7** The Queen Vic **8** He beat up Graham **9** Jean **10** Dr Anthony Trueman **11** Iron **12** Lynne **13** Bert Atkinson **14** Dawn Swan **15** Zoe Slater **16** Belinda **17** Andy Hunter **18** Mo **19** Dr Oliver Cousins **20** Spencer Moon

QUIZ 28
Page 60

Sharon Watts Answers

1 Grant **2** Vicki and Dennis **3** The Banned **4** False – she was adopted **5** Princess **6** Dennis **7** On a tape **8** Angie's Den **9** Tom Banks **10** False **11** Vicar **12** America **13** The Queen Vic **14** Trevor Morgan **15** Cindy **16** True **17** Grant Mitchell **18** Danny Moon **19** Phil and Kathy's **20** Letitia Dean

QUIZ 29
Page 62

EastEnders Deaths Answers

1 Den Watts **2** Frank Butcher **3** Nick Cotton **4** He was pushed off a cliff by Janine **5** Cot death **6** Jamie **7** Reg Cox **8** Phil Mitchell **9** He fell from a window **10** Andy Hunter **11** Laura Beale **12** An ash tray **13** Tom Banks **14** Danny Moon **15** Mark Fowler's **16** A brain haemorrhage **17** Ethel Skinner **18** Cindy Beale **19** She jumped from a roof **20** False – he had a heart attack

QUIZ 30
Page 64

Emmerdale The 1970s Answers

1 1972 **2** A funeral **3** True **4** Sharon Crossthwaite **5** George Verney **6** False – she was called Marion **7** School caretaker **8** Dolly **9** Sam and Sally **10** The Woolpack **11** Ian 'Trash' McIntyre **12** Joe Sugden **13** Vicar **14** Peggy Skilbeck **15** Christine **16** Amos Brearley **17** Jimmy **18** Subsidence **19** False – it was NY Estates **20** Mrs McClusky in *Grange Hill*

QUIZ 31

Page 66

Emmerdale The 1980s Answers

1 Rome 2 Dolly 3 Jackie Merrick 4 Enoch Tolly 5 At the mobile library 6 Amos Brearley 7 The Malt Shovel 8 Meg 9 Vet 10 Alan Turner 11 Mark Hughes 12 Auctioneer 13 He brought out his ferret 14 A nuclear waste dump 15 Jackie Merrick 16 Sandie Merrick 17 Nick Bates 18 Ross Kemp 19 True 20 Frank Tate

QUIZ 32

Page 68

Emmerdale The 1990s Answers

1 Spain 2 Neil Kincaid 3 Dee de la Cruz 4 Bernice Blackstock 5 Interior designer 6 Charlie Aindow 7 Nick Bates 8 Roy 9 She touched up her lipstick 10 True 11 Ian Botham 12 The Munch Box 13 Debbie Wilson 14 Alan Turner (his wife Shirley was killed) 15 Kathy Tate 16 Emma Cairns 17 Terry Woods 18 Kate Hughes 19 Tampered with his brakes 20 Alan Turner

QUIZ 33

Page 70

Emmerdale Modern Day Answers

1 Cathy and Heathcliff 2 Paddy Kirk 3 Cancer 4 Billy Hopwood 5 In a barn 6 Paddy Kirk (one), Bob Hope (one) 7 *The Jeremy Kyle Show* 8 A priest 9 Toni Daggert 10 Len Reynolds 11 Dan McHerron 12 Jamie Hope 13 A goat 14 Victoria Sugden 15 Shadrach 16 An internet get rich quick scheme 17 Kelly Windsor 18 The Cardigans 19 Carl King 20 Val Lambert

QUIZ 34

Page 72

Emmerdale Deaths Answers

1 Tricia Dingle 2 The plane crash 3 Jacob Sugden 4 Frank Tate 5 In a fire 6 Zoe Tate 7 Butch 8 Dave Glover 9 Charity 10 He fell and hit his head after being pushed down the stairs 11 Eric Pollard 12 Grace Barraclough 13 Billy Hopwood 14 Graham Clark 15 Angie Reynolds 16 Snort cocaine 17 Graham Clark 18 True 19 Sam Dingle 20 Dawn Woods, Noreen Bell and David Brown

QUIZ 35

Page 74

Around Emmerdale Answers

1 Yorkshire 2 The Woolpack 3 The Dingles 4 Beckindale 5 Kathy Glover 6 Woodbine 7 Archie Hill is named after Archie Brooks 8 St Mary's 9 The Vet's 10 The Grange 11 Keeper's Cottage 12 Eric Pollard 13 Pear Tree Cottage 14 Chez Marlon 15 Paul Marsden 16 The Tates 17 Hotten 18 Scott Windsor and Debbie Dingle 19 The Windsors 20 Frank Tate

QUIZ 36

Page 76

The Dingles Answers
1 Belle 2 Angie Reynolds 3 Mandy 4 Chastity Dingle 5 Samson
6 Chastity and Cain 7 Marlon 8 Brothers 9 Chastity Dingle
10 Josiah 11 He was involved in a bus crash 12 Wishing Well Cottage
13 Testicular 14 Marlon 15 Edna Birch 16 Charity 17 Ned Glover
18 Marlon 19 Barry 20 Tom Cruise Dingle

QUIZ 37

Page 78

The Kings Answers
1 Jimmy 2 Chastity 3 Vet 4 Charity 5 Colleen 6 Scarlett Nicholls
7 Postman 8 He fell from scaffolding 9 Anya and Thomas 10 Jimmy
11 Kelly Windsor 12 Louise Appleton 13 Sadie 14 Edna Birch
15 Chloe Atkinson 16 In a car crash 17 Grace Barraclough 18 Carl
and Matthew King 19 Scott Windsor 20 Carl King

QUIZ 38

Page 80

The Sugdens Answers
1 Annie 2 In detention at school 3 He was accidentally shot
4 Librarian 5 True 6 Robert Sugden 7 Butler's Farm 8 Andy 9 True
10 Sarah 11 Andy 12 Hitting a tutor with a canoe paddle 13 Billy
Hopwood 14 Max King 15 Debbie Dingle 16 Joe Sugden 17 Rachel
Hughes 18 Cancer 19 Amos Brearley 20 Clive Hornby

QUIZ 39

Page 82

Hollyoaks The Early Years Answers
1 1995 2 Chester 3 Kurt 4 Brian 5 Rory 'Finn' Finnigan 6 Anna
Green 7 Jambo 8 Mandy Richardson 9 Steam Team 10 Kate Patrick
11 Car crash 12 Emily 13 Jambo 14 Natasha Anderson 15 Rob
Hawthorne 16 Maddie Parker 17 Dennis 18 Cindy Cunningham
19 Mark Gibbs 20 She was psychic

QUIZ 40

Page 84

Hollyoaks The New Millennium Answers
1 Neville Ashworth 2 Matt Musgrove 3 Luke Morgan 4 Theo Sankofa
and Jamie Nash 5 Beauty Therapy 6 Policeman 7 Bella Manning
8 Ellie Hunter 9 A pork scratching 10 Sam Owen 11 Justin Burton
12 Steph Dean 13 Manchester City 14 America 15 Fireman
16 Steven 'Macki' Mackintosh 17 Obsessive Compulsive Disorder
18 Dan Hunter 19 Bombhead 20 Warren Fox

Answers from pages 76-85

QUIZ 41
Page 86

Hollyoaks The Modern Era Answers
1 John Paul McQueen **2** Elliot Bevan **3** Steph Dean **4** Justin Burton **5** Charlie **6** Bulimia/Anorexia **7** Warren Fox **8** Albania **9** Nancy Hayton and Hannah Ashworth **10** Will Hackett **11** Foz **12** She was stabbed by her prison cellmate, Fran **13** Ste Hay **14** Mercedes McQueen **15** The Baby Diegos **16** False – it was a donkey **17** His girlfriend Katy **18** Will Hackett **19** France **20** Brian Belo

QUIZ 42
Page 88

Max and OB Answers
1 Clare Devine **2** Sam O'Brien **3** The Loft **4** Tom **5** Burger van **6** Mel Burton **7** Gordon Cunningham **8** False – OB saved Max **9** Taking cocaine **10** In a car crash **11** Chloe **12** True **13** Alcohol **14** Clare Devine **15** They were selling junk food **16** True **17** MOBS **18** Steph Dean **19** Matt Littler (Ben Sheriff also played the role, from 1995 to 1997) **20** Darren Jeffries

QUIZ 43
Page 90

Tony Hutchinson Answers
1 Chef **2** Dom **3** Jacqui McQueen **4** Julie **5** Taxi driver **6** Got It Taped **7** Carol **8** Andy **9** Helen Cunningham **10** Gnosh **11** Lucy Benson **12** Lewis Richardson **13** Tessie **14** True **15** Finn **16** Julie and Izzy **17** Rome **18** A septic tank **19** Grace **20** Nick Pickard

QUIZ 44
Page 92

The McQueens Answers
1 Five **2** Marjorie **3** Jacqui, Tina, Carmel, Michaela and Mercedes **4** Tina and Mercedes **5** At his girlfriend's 18th birthday party **6** Mercedes **7** Aleksander Malota **8** Spike **9** Sophie Burton **10** Wayne Tunnicliffe **11** Dublin **12** Craig Dean **13** A wakeboard **14** Warren **15** Carbon monoxide **16** Warren **17** Tina **18** Liverpool **19** Carmel **20** Carmel

QUIZ 45
Page 94

Home and Away The First 10 Years Answers
1 1989 **2** Frank Morgan, Carly Morris, Steven Matheson, Lynn Davenport and Sally **3** Floss **4** A hair and beauty salon **5** Alan **6** Michael Ross **7** Jack Wilson **8** Lance **9** James **10** Sophie Simpson **11** Alf **12** Bobby **13** Tug **14** Jack **15** Saul Bennett **16** Brian 'Dodge' Forbes **17** An earthquake **18** Brad Cooper **19** Actress **20** Travis and Rebecca

QUIZ 46
Page 96

Home and Away The New Millennium Answers
1 Jade 2 Paris Burnett 3 Woody 4 The Believers 5 Hawaiian shirts
6 Eve Jacobsen (Zoe McCallister) 7 They are all cops 8 Robbie
9 Project 56 10 Angie Russell 11 Vinnie Patterson 12 True 13 Sarah
Lewis 14 He bought a stolen exam paper 15 Gus Phillips 16 Viv
Anderson 17 Edward Dunglass 18 Strip poker 19 Corey Henderson
20 VJ (Vincent Junior)

QUIZ 47
Page 98

Home and Away The Modern Age Answers
1 Ric Dalby 2 Cancer 3 Cassie Turner 4 Amanda Baker and Belle
Taylor 5 Ash Nader 6 Tony and Lucas Holden 7 Drew Curtis
8 America 9 Roo Stewart 10 He was really gay 11 Peter Baker
12 True 13 The Rocket Club 14 Cameron Reynolds 15 Milco
16 Drew Curtis 17 In a car crash 18 Sam Tolhurst 19 She spiked a
drink 20 Drugs possession

QUIZ 48
Page 100

Home and Away Deaths Answers
1 Boating accident 2 Dylan 3 Saul Bennett 4 Heart attack 5 Sarah
Lewis 6 Alf Stewart's 7 Rory Heywood 8 She ran in front of a train
9 Donald Fisher's 10 Geoff Campbell 11 Shane 12 Marc Edwards
13 Jesse McGregor 14 Michael Ross 15 Barry Hyde 16 Robbie
Hunter 17 Felix Walters 18 Heart attack 19 Skin 20 A cliff

QUIZ 49
Page 102

Around Summer Bay Answers
1 Sydney 2 The Beachside Diner 3 The Beach House 4 Noah Lawson
5 Five 6 Super Bods 7 Alf Stewart 8 The Diner 9 Yabbie Creek
10 Alf and Ailsa Stewart 11 St James' 12 Palm Beach 13 Brothel
14 Jesse McGregor 15 Angie 16 The Surf Club 17 Stripper
18 Donald Fisher 19 Lucas 20 Vinnie Patterson

QUIZ 50
Page 104

Donald Fisher Answers
1 Teacher 2 Alf Stewart – his sister was Barbara 3 Isobel 4 Hayley
Smith 5 Flathead 6 Surfing 7 Travis 8 Bobby 9 Morag Bellingham
10 Being involved in a sit-in at school 11 Seb 12 Marilyn Chambers
13 June Reynolds 14 True 15 Cancer 16 Nick Parrish 17 The
Olympic Torch 18 Hotel 19 *A Letter To Byron* 20 Norman Coburn

QUIZ 51

Page 106

Sally Fletcher Answers
1 Flynn Saunders 2 Pippa 3 Kieran 4 Dan 5 Milko 6 True 7 Boating accident 8 Cassie Turner 9 Diesel 10 Ric Dalby 11 Alf 12 Leah 13 History 14 Bonza Burgers 15 Archaeology 16 Ovarian cancer 17 Brad 18 Zoe McAllister/Eve Jacobson 19 Stab her 20 Kate Ritchie

QUIZ 52

Page 108

Alf Stewart Answers
1 Martha and Ailsa 2 Alf and Jesse's Baits and Bits Store 3 Fraud 4 Duncan 5 Donald Fisher 6 The Blaxland 7 Pippa 8 Martha 9 True 10 Douglas 11 Heart attack 12 Roo 13 False 14 Coin 15 The Summer Bay Life Saving Team 16 True 17 Ric 18 Four 19 Morag, Barbara, Celia and Debra 20 Ray Meagher

QUIZ 53

Page 110

Neighbours The 1980s Answers
1 1986 2 Doctor 3 Maria 4 Mike Young 5 Charlene 6 Cricket 7 Mrs Mangel 8 A Gorillagram 9 Melanie Pearson 10 Bank Manager 11 Shane Ramsay 12 Terry 13 Mrs Mangel 14 Jamie 15 Mrs Mangel 16 Lucy Robinson 17 Henry Ramsay 18 Bronwyn and Sharon Davies 19 Helen Daniels 20 Katie

QUIZ 54

Page 112

Neighbours The 1990s Answers
1 Madge and Harold 2 Tad 3 Christina 4 Guy 5 The Holy Roll 6 Ballroom dancing 7 Pam Willis 8 Ruth Wilkinson 9 Annalise Hartman and Gaby Willis 10 Eddie Buckingham 11 Joe Mangel and Melanie Pearson 12 Hope 13 Philip Martin 14 Kenya 15 Erinsborough High School 16 Mike Healey 17 True 18 Beth Brennan 19 The Scully's 20 Susan Kennedy

QUIZ 55

Page 114

Neighbours Present Day Answers
1 Pouch 2 Stingray 3 A fire at the hospital 4 Helicopter 5 Max Hoyland 6 Kirsten 7 Guy Sykes 8 Toadfish 9 An Aussie Rules football team 10 Carmella Cammeniti 11 Emma Bunton 12 Mary Casey 13 1940s 14 Terrence Chesterton 15 Sky Mangel and Lana Crawford 16 True 17 He was trampled by a horse 18 The Beatles 19 To find her granddaughter 20 Madge's cookbook

QUIZ 56
Page 116

Neighbours Deaths Answers
1 Heart attack **2** Daphne Clarke **3** He was thrown from a horse
4 Paris **5** Reuben White **6** Karl Kennedy **7** He was murdered **8** Kerry
Bishop **9** In a plane crash **10** Harold Bishop **11** Gary Briggs **12** Car
crash **13** Helen Daniels **14** Lily Madigan **15** Todd Landers **16** Cody
17 Brendan **18** Julie Martin **19** Toby Mangel **20** Alex Kinski

QUIZ 57
Page 118

Around Erinsborough Answers
1 Melbourne **2** Ramsay Street **3** Rosemary Daniels **4** Charlie's
5 The Waterhole **6** Grease Monkeys **7** Basketball **8** The Coffee Shop
9 Bounce **10** Warrinor Prison **11** Uni FM **12** Cheryl Stark **13** Purple
14 Carpenter's Mechanics **15** A Good Hair Day **16** The House of
Trouser **17** West Waratah Caravan Park **18** *The News* **19** Heartbridge
20 26

QUIZ 58
Page 120

Harold and Lou Answers
1 Paul Robinson **2** Lolly **3** Three **4** Cathy, Linda and Trixie **5** Sky
6 Jelly Belly **7** Mrs Mangel **8** Guy, Lauren and Ling Mai **9** False –
Harold donated a kidney to Lou **10** Tasmania **11** Kerry and David
12 Mishka **13** Dungeons and Dragons **14** Ted **15** Annalise Hartman
16 Lori and Connor **17** Reverend Rosie Hoyland **18** Tad Reeves and
Paul McClain **19** Ian Smith **20** Tom Oliver

QUIZ 59
Page 122

The Kennedys Answers
1 Doctor **2** Tom **3** Teacher **4** Three **5** Drew Kirk **6** Lou Carpenter
7 Sarah Beaumont **8** Darcy **9** Carpenter **10** Father Tom Scully
11 She banged her head after slipping on some milk **12** Ben **13** Alex
Kinski **14** Izzy Hoyland **15** Smith **16** Neil Morrissey **17** Cuppa Diem
18 True **19** The London Eye **20** Sinitta

QUIZ 60
Page 124

The Robinsons Answers
1 Helen Daniels **2** Charlene Ramsay **3** Dr Beverley Marshall
4 Amy, Cameron, Lucinda (Elle), Robert and Andrew **5** Gail **6** Paul
7 Paul **8** Philip Martin **9** Lucy **10** Robert Robinson **11** Max Hoyland
12 Ned Parker **13** Glen **14** He was thrown from a cliff **15** Mr Udagawa
16 Nick Page **17** Fox **18** Fiona Hartman **19** Paul **20** Alan Dale

QUIZ 61
Page 126

Brookside Part One Answers
1 Liverpool **2** Sinbad **3** Under the patio **4** Sheila **5** Tommy McArdle **6** The Moby **7** Simon **8** Beth Jordache and Margaret Clemence **9** La Luz **10** Georgia Simpson **11** Rosie Banks **12** Ron Dixon **13** A bomb exploded **14** Mick Johnson **15** Anna Friel **16** She fell down the stairs **17** Imelda Clough **18** Bernie **19** Gordon Collins **20** Jennifer Ellison

QUIZ 62
Page 128

Brookside Part Two Answers
1 Mike, Jacqui and Tony **2** Graham Norton **3** Patricia, Susannah and Jacqui **4** Damon **5** Shifty **6** Priest **7** Harry Cross **8** Christian **9** Jacqui Dixon **10** She fell from a window **11** Anthony Murray **12** Colin Jackson **13** Nikki **14** Geoff Rogers **15** False, but his *Through The Keyhole* co-star did make a cameo appearance **16** Mike Dixon **17** Callum Finnegan **18** Nicholas Black **19** A Harley-Davidson motorbike **20** *Grange Hill*

QUIZ 63
Page 130

The Corkhills Answers
1 Brothers **2** Drugs **3** Jackie **4** Billy **5** Lindsey, 'Little' Jimmy and William **6** Policeman **7** Peter Phelan **8** Kowboy Kutz **9** Sheila **10** Korky Kars **11** Hairdresser **12** Ron Dixon **13** Cracker **14** Frank Rogers **15** Kylie **16** Diana **17** Shelley **18** Lindsey **19** False – he was a history teacher **20** Dean Sullivan

QUIZ 64
Page 132

Crossroads Answers
1 Birmingham **2** A woolly hat **3** 1960s **4** Meg Richardson **5** David and Barbara **6** Miss Diane **7** Sue Nicholls **8** A fire **9** Kathy Staff **10** Malcolm Ryder **11** True **12** The QE2 **13** Adam **14** True **15** Jane Asher **16** Jill Chance **17** Ronnie Barker **18** King's Oak **19** Wings **20** Harold Wilson

QUIZ 65
Page 134

Dallas Answers
1 Texas **2** The Ewings and the Barnes's **3** Larry Hagman **4** Southfork **5** Bobby Ewing **6** Cliff Barnes **7** Four – J.R., Bobby and Gary Ewing and Ray Krebbs **8** Sue Ellen **9** True – he played Charlie's boyfriend **10** Miss Ellie **11** Nicholas Pearce **12** Clayton Farlow **13** Lucy **14** Digger **15** John Ross **16** Road accident **17** Lucy **18** Bobby Ewing **19** Linda Evans **20** Kristin Shepherd

QUIZ 66

Page 136

Dynasty Answers

1 Denver 2 Stephanie Beacham 3 The Carringtons 4 Krystle 5 True
6 Alexis 7 Heather Locklear 8 Stephen 9 False – but former US
President Gerald Ford did appear 10 Adam Carrington 11 Moldavia
12 Caress 13 Fallon 14 True 15 Michael Praed 16 Oil 17 Alexis
18 Alexis's art studio 19 Allegre 20 Adam Carrington

QUIZ 67

Page 138

Eldorado Answers

1 Spain 2 Trish Valentine 3 Marcus Tandy 4 One year 5 Los Barcos
6 Wogan 7 Georgio's 8 Drew 9 156 10 Charlie Slater 11 True
12 *Go Away* 13 Pilar 14 He played policeman DCI Charlie Mason
15 True 16 Fizz 17 The Butlers 18 Joy's Bar 19 Nessa and Blair
20 Cassandra

QUIZ 68

Page 140

Family Affairs Answers

1 Channel 5 2 Helen Hart 3 The Black Swan 4 Stanley Street 5 Pete
Callan 6 Liam 7 Charnham 8 Susie Ross 9 Cat 10 Yasmin Green
11 Dusty McHugh 12 The Davenport family 13 The Lock 14 Roy
Farmer 15 Peter Stringfellow 16 Pete Callan 17 Serge Pompidou
18 Taxi driver 19 *Minder* 20 Vince Farmer

QUIZ 69

Page 142

Prisoner Cell Block H Answers

1 Wentworth Detention Centre 2 Ann Reynolds 3 Colleen Powell
4 Sonia Stevens 5 Joan Ferguson 6 Lizzie Birdsworth 7 Top Dog
8 Nola Mckenzie 9 Jim Fletcher 10 Barbara Fields 11 Bea Smith
12 The Freak 13 Chef 14 Vera Bennett 15 Teddy bear 16 Phyllis
Hunt 17 Meg Jackson (Morris) 18 Nana 19 True 20 *On The Inside*

QUIZ 70

Page 144

Actors Answers

1 G 2 M 3 I 4 R 5 K 6 Q 7 C 8 O 9 P 10 B 11 E 12 D 13 N
14 A 15 T 16 S 17 H 18 J 19 F 20 L

QUIZ 71

Page 146

Affairs Part One Answers
1 Deirdre 2 Izzy Hoyland 3 Cindy 4 Ken Barlow 5 Tracy Barlow
6 Tony Hutchinson 7 Dennis Stringer 8 Dan Sullivan 9 Cassie Turner
10 Matt Ramsden 11 Finn 12 Arthur Fowler 13 Linda Sykes 14 Kelly
Windsor 15 Vicar 16 Sally Webster 17 Carlos 18 Kate 19 Max
Branning 20 Rebecca Hopkins

QUIZ 72

Page 148

Affairs Part Two Answers
1 Videotape 2 Kevin Webster 3 Natalie 4 Guy Carpenter 5 Michael
Rose 6 Audrey Roberts 7 Pat and Patrick's 8 Frankie Baldwin 9 Troy
10 Max Branning 11 Tim 12 A revolving bow tie 13 Brett Stark
14 Grant 15 Spain 16 Peter Baker 17 Frankie 18 Den Watts
19 Meena 20 Patrice

QUIZ 73

Page 150

Animal Magic Answers
1 Roly 2 Sheep 3 Jack Duckworth 4 Drew Kirk 5 Cat 6 Suede Tess
7 Cain Dingle 8 Ethel Skinner 9 Ozzy 10 Phoebe 11 Batley
12 A rabbit 13 Colonel Parker 14 Schmeichel 15 Wellard 16 True
17 Kim Tate 18 Abi Branning 19 Budgie 20 A parrot called Corky

QUIZ 74

Page 152

Babes Answers
1 Roxanne McKee 2 Annalise Hartman 3 Michelle Connor 4 Harry
Kewell 5 Shannon Reed 6 Karen McDonald 7 Jo Stiles 8 Debbie Dean
9 Beth Brennan 10 Grant 11 Emily Shadwick 12 Lisa Hunter
13 Blackpool Tower 14 Flick Scully 15 Izzy Cornwell 16 Max
Branning 17 Linda Lusardi 18 Pepper 19 Rosie Webster 20 Jessie
Wallace

QUIZ 75

Page 154

Bad Boys Answers
1 Nick 2 Kane Phillips 3 Alan Bradley 4 Cain Dingle 5 Robert
Robinson 6 Trevor Morgan 7 Jez Quigley 8 Footballer 9 Graham Clark
10 Dan Sullivan 11 Barry Grant 12 Aiden Critchley 13 Steve Owen
14 Brazil 15 Zoe Carpenter 16 James Wilmott-Brown 17 George
Palmer 18 Duggie Ferguson 19 Fraud 20 Johnny Allen

QUIZ 76

Page 156

Behind The Bar Answers

1 Ciaran McCarthy **2** Diane Sugden and Val Lambert **3** Noah's Bar **4** The Dog In The Pond **5** Jack Osborne **6** Bev Unwin **7** Henry Wilks **8** Fred Gee **9** Hilda Ogden **10** Tricia Dingle **11** Bar Brookie **12** Jacqui Farnham **13** Teresa di Marco **14** Alfie Moon **15** Tricia Stokes/Dingle **16** Michelle Connor **17** Sean Slater **18** Bernice Blackstock **19** Mel and Sophie Burton, Joe, Olivia and Sam **20** The Gatsby Club

QUIZ 77

Page 158

Bitches Answers

1 She pushed him off a cliff **2** Alexis Colby **3** Lawyer **4** Her OCD pills **5** Kelly Windsor **6** Elle Robinson **7** Kate Patrick **8** She was pregnant **9** Steph Stokes **10** Paul Trueman **11** Dev Alahan **12** Footballer **13** Italy **14** In a helicopter **15** Sharon **16** Sadie King **17** Karen McDonald **18** Jasmine Thomas **19** A horse **20** Katy Fox

QUIZ 78

Page 160

Blondes Answers

1 Sharon **2** Maxine Peacock **3** Raquel **4** Kim Tate **5** Dee Bliss **6** Ian Beale **7** Rachel **8** Geri Hudson for Izzy Cornwell **9** Cindy Beale **10** Natalie Horrocks **11** Becca Dean **12** Film director **13** Mrs Mangel **14** Amanda Baker **15** Ronnie and Roxy **16** Emily O'Leary **17** Bet Lynch **18** Dave Glover **19** Lisa Hunter **20** Steph Dean

QUIZ 79

Page 162

Brothers and Sisters Answers

1 Max Cunningham **2** Caroline and Christina **3** Beppe, Gianni, Teresa and Nicky **4** Jodie, Mel, Kayleigh and Darryl **5** Tony Hutchinson and Dominic Reilly **6** Paul, Lucy, Scott and Julie and his long lost son Glen Donnelly **7** Georgia and Nat Simpson **8** Malcolm, Libby and Billy Kennedy and Holly Hoyland **9** Ken Barlow **10** Natalie Horrocks **11** The car they were travelling in was struck by a train **12** Val Lambert **13** Ronnie and Roxy Mitchell **14** Katya Kinski **15** William and Rebecca **16** Nita **17** Emma Jackson **18** *Doctors* **19** Steve **20** Dawn, Jude, Cindy, Max and Tom

QUIZ 80

Page 164

Crime Answers

1 Toby Mills **2** The Firm **3** He streaked at a football match **4** A statue **5** Rocco Cammeniti **6** Liz McDonald **7** Vinnie Patterson **8** Jim McDonald **9** Clare Devine **10** Aiden Critchley **11** False – it was a statue of a horse's head **12** Scott Anderson **13** Daffodils **14** Bethany Platt **15** Paul Usher **16** Precious **17** Ernest Bishop **18** Matthew Rose **19** Johnny Allen **20** Casey Carswell

QUIZ 81

Page 166

Golden Oldies Answers
1 The London Eye **2** Betty Turpin **3** Ken Barlow **4** Jules **5** Betty Eagleton **6** Phyllis Pearce **7** Helen Daniels **8** The launderette **9** Pat **10** Nellie **11** Seth **12** Hilda Ogden **13** Gambling **14** Maud **15** Edna Birch **16** Lollipop man **17** Wally Bannister **18** Selling duty-free cigarettes **19** Eileen **20** Amos Brearley

QUIZ 82

Page 168

Grumpy Old Men Answers
1 Albert Tatlock **2** Charlie **3** Gamekeeper **4** Percy Sugden **5** Bruce **6** Stan Ogden **7** Harry Cross **8** Norris Cole **9** Renee **10** Shadrach Dingle **11** Harry Slater **12** Barman **13** Terry **14** Eric Pollard **15** Charlie Slater **16** Fred Gee **17** Alf Roberts **18** Doug Willis **19** Derek Harkinson **20** Rob Lewis

QUIZ 83

Page 170

Guest Appearances Answers
1 Prince Charles **2** Heather Mills **3** A priest **4** Katherine Jenkins **5** Sir Norman Wisdom **6** *Neighbours* **7** *Coronation Street* **8** Darius **9** Michael Parkinson **10** Melvin Hutchwright **11** *Emmerdale* **12** False – David Walliams has appeared in the show though **13** Lleyton Hewitt **14** Peter Kay **15** Atomic Kitten **16** Emma Bunton **17** True **18** Shane Warne **19** Tony Christie **20** Michael Palin

QUIZ 84

Page 172

Hunks Answers
1 Liam Connor **2** Dev Alahan **3** Police officer **4** Paul Lambert **5** Zoe Slater **6** Rachel Armstrong **7** David Metcalfe **8** Brian Tilsley **9** Sandra **10** Ned Parker **11** Dave Glover **12** Lisa **13** Cain Dingle **14** Farmer **15** *Strictly Come Dancing* **16** Craig Harris **17** Oakey **18** Ben Davies **19** Justin Burton **20** Joe

QUIZ 85

Page 174

Life After Soaps Answers
1 Nick Berry **2** Guy Pearce **3** *Cutting It* **4** Ross Kemp **5** *Vincent* **6** Todd Carty **7** Alan Dale **8** *Casualty* **9** *Harbour Lights* **10** *Hollyoaks* **11** Russell Crowe **12** *Footballers' Wives* **13** Tamsin Outhwaite **14** Des Taviner **15** *Keeping Up Appearances* **16** Mark Little **17** The Royle Family **18** Anna Friel **19** *Two Pints of Lager and a Packet of Crisps Please* **20** Isla Fisher

QUIZ 86
Page 176

Life Before Soaps Answers
1 Barbara Windsor 2 Una Stubbs 3 Phil Daniels 4 Hear'say 5 True
6 Samantha Janus 7 Paul Usher 8 Guy Pearce 9 Keith Barron
10 Miss Brahms 11 Patsy Kensit 12 Ken Masters 13 Lorraine Chase
14 Boon 15 Spandau Ballet 16 Private Pike 17 Goldie 18 *EastEnders*
19 *Bergerac* 20 Honor Blackman

QUIZ 87
Page 178

Match The Character Answers
1 *EastEnders* 2 *Emmerdale* 3 *Dallas* 4 *Coronation Street*
5 *Neighbours* 6 *EastEnders* 7 *Coronation Street* 8 *Dynasty* 9 *Home
and Away* 10 *Brookside* 11 *Coronation Street* 12 *Neighbours*
13 *Crossroads* 14 *Neighbours* 15 *Crossroads* 16 *Neighbours*
17 *EastEnders* 18 *Dallas* 19 *Coronation Street* 20 *Emmerdale*

QUIZ 88
Page 180

Matriarchs Answers
1 Lou Beale 2 Ivy Tilsley 3 Mo Harris 4 Madge 5 Pippa Fletcher
6 Helen Daniels 7 Mo 8 Amy 9 Scott, Donna, Heath and Cathy
10 Lou Beale 11 Annie Sugden 12 Adam, Cody, Brad and Gaby
13 Irene Roberts 14 Peggy Mitchell 15 Rosie and Sophie
16 Cheryl Stark 17 Carol Jackson 18 Lyn Scully 19 Myra McQueen
20 Phyllis Pearce

QUIZ 89
Page 182

Medical Matters Answers
1 Dr Legg 2 Pam Willis 3 Dr Flynn Saunders 4 Martin Platt 5 Dr Clive
Gibbons 6 Dr Darcy Tyler 7 Sonia 8 Dr Oliver Cousins 9 Dr Trueman
10 True 11 Fire extinguisher 12 Maxine Peacock 13 Car crash
14 Dr Fonseca 15 Andy O'Brien 16 Vera Duckworth 17 Steph
18 Martin Platt 19 Dr May Wright 20 Billy Kennedy played by
Jesse Spencer

QUIZ 90
Page 184

Merry Christmas Answers
1 Arthur Fowler 2 Deirdre Barlow 3 Tom King 4 Stephen 5 David
Platt 6 Grant Mitchell 7 Louise Appleton 8 Phil Mitchell 9 Steve
10 Bianca 11 Claire Casey 12 Danny Moon 13 Ivy Tilsley 14 Mandy
Salter 15 Vic Windsor 16 Pat Butcher 17 Don Brennan's taxi
18 Kim's 19 Jason Grimshaw 20 Grant Mitchell

QUIZ 91
Page 186

More Than One Soap Answers
1 Graham Lodsworth 2 Mike Baldwin 3 *Crossroads* 4 Louise Appleton
5 Jambo 6 Letitia Dean 7 Clare Tyler 8 Julie Peasgood 9 Gloria Todd
10 Rebecca Hopkins 11 Foz 12 Jim Robinson 13 Tina Fowler
14 *Brookside* 15 Max Farnham 16 Matt Musgrove 17 Lily Butterfield
18 *Brookside* 19 Sam Kane 20 *EastEnders*

QUIZ 92
Page 188

Nicknames Answers
1 Tinhead 2 Curly 3 Toadfish 4 Lofty 5 Jambo 6 Bombhead 7 Tug
8 Stonefish 9 Bing 10 Spider 11 Squiggle 12 Tricky Dicky 13 OB
14 Plain Jane Superbrain 15 Button 16 Sinbad 17 Wicksy 18 Dirty
Den 19 Biff 20 Mincemeat

QUIZ 93
Page 189

Occupations Answers
1 F 2 P 3 K 4 A 5 Q 6 H 7 J 8 T 9 B 10 C 11 D 12 S 13 R 14 E
15 G 16 I 17 L 18 M 19 N 20 O

QUIZ 94
Page 190

Parents Answers
1 Roy Cropper 2 David Metcalfe 3 Brian Wicks 4 Michelle Fowler
5 Bill Kenwright 6 False – Frank Tate was the father 7 Rosie, Sophie
and the deceased Jake 8 Cindy Cunningham 9 Jack 10 Libby Kennedy
11 Jamie 12 Neil Fearns 13 Leah Patterson 14 Tracy Barlow
15 Samson 16 Alex 17 Courtney Mitchell and Mark Fowler Junior
18 Garry Hobbs 19 the bookmakers 20 Byron

QUIZ 95
Page 192

Quotations Answers
1 *EastEnders* 2 Violet 3 Harold Bishop 4 Ken Barlow 5 Flaming galah
6 Den Watts 7 Pauline Fowler 8 Sarah-Louise Platt 9 Clare Devine
10 Shadrach Dingle 11 Eileen Grimshaw 12 Johnny Allen
13 Mike Baldwin 14 Pat 15 Eric Pollard 16 Richard Hillman
17 Den Watts 18 Jim McDonald 19 Zara 20 Dot Cotton

QUIZ 96 Page 194

Reality TV Answers
1 Claire Sweeney 2 *Celebrity Fit Club* 3 Dean Martin 4 Will Mellor
5 Jocelyn Brown 6 *The Match* 7 Kimberley Davies 8 *The Games*
9 Matt di Angelo 10 *Showbiz Darts* 11 They all appeared on
I'm a Celebrity Get Me Out of Here 12 Barbara Windsor 13 Nadia
Sawalha 14 *Soapstar Superstar* 15 Patsy Palmer 16 *Celebrity Shark
Bait* 17 Todd Carty 18 *Celebrity Love Island* 19 Adam Rickitt
20 Meatloaf

QUIZ 97 Page 196

Singing Soap Stars Answers
1 Kylie Minogue 2 False 3 Martine McCutcheon 4 Madonna 5 Stefan
Dennis 6 True 7 Goldie 8 Tony Hatch 9 Robbie Williams 10 Brian
May 11 Nick Berry 12 *Home and Away* 13 Martin Kemp 14 The
Woolpackers 15 Perry Como 16 Michelle Gayle 17 Lee Otway aka
Bombhead 18 Nina Tucker 19 Mona 20 *Something Outta Nothing*

QUIZ 98 Page 198

Spin Offs and Specials Answers
1 Blackpool 2 *Brookside* 3 True 4 *EastEnders* 5 Curly and Raquel
6 Alec Gilroy 7 Australia 8 *Brookside* 9 Vicky Arden's 10 Morrissey
11 Expression 12 Ben and Lisa 13 True 14 The Mitchells 15 *Dallas*
16 Jack and Vera Duckworth 17 Venice 18 The Slaters 19 The Colbys
20 Wendy Richard and Adam Woodyatt

QUIZ 99 Page 200

Wedding Bells Answers
1 Scott Robinson and Charlene Mitchell 2 Phil Mitchell and Stella
Crawford's 3 Sadie King 4 Ray Langton 5 Trixie 6 Shelly Unwin
7 Mo Slater 8 Kat Slater 9 Les and Cilla Battersby-Brown 10 He lied
about his daughter's cancer 11 Daphne Clarke 12 Roy's Rolls
13 Bob Hope 14 Drew Kirk 15 *We're All Going on a Summer Holiday*
16 Frazer and Rosa Yeats 17 Des Clarke's 18 The hospital 19 David
Platt 20 Julie

QUIZ 100 Page 202

Weren't They in The Bill? Answers
1 K 2 Q 3 E 4 M 5 H 6 C 7 J 8 T 9 F 10 A 11 I 12 S 13 B 14 U
15 D 16 G 17 L 18 N 19 O 20 R